MOSTLY PLANT-BASED

Platters
&Boards

MOSTLY PLANT-BASED

Platters &Boards

Gorgeous Spreads for Clean Eating + Great Gatherings
Lea Dixon, The Platter Girl

CASTLE POINT BOOKS

NEW YORK

www.castlepointbooks.com

The Castle Point Books trademark is owned by Castle Point Publishing, LLC.
Castle Point books are published and distributed by St. Martin's Publishing Group.

ISBN 978-1-250-28225-5 (paper over board)
ISBN 978-1-250-28385-6 (ebook)

Design by Tara Long
Photography by Lea Dixon, except page 9 (Ian Pitts) and pages 24, 62, 100, and 126
(Cody Keto Photography)

Our books may be purchased in bulk for promotional, educational, or business use.
Please contact your local bookseller or the Macmillan Corporate and Premium Sales Department
at 1-800-221-7945, extension 5442, or by email at MacmillanSpecialMarkets@macmillan.com.

First Edition: 2023

10 9 8 7 6 5 4 3 2 1

**To my cheese squad
making amazing grazing creations—
you inspire me every single day.**

Contents

WELCOME TO THE BOARD **8**

PLATTER MAGIC **11**

ANYTIME GRAZING **24**

SALAD SPREADS **62**

HOT PLATTERS **76**

SWEETS & CELEBRATIONS **100**

FINISHING TOUCHES **126**

INDEX **154**

Welcome to the Board

Have you ever been in love? It must have been 2017 scrolling through "pins" when I fell hard and fast for an amazing grazing board. The abundance of glorious snacks . . . the insane array of colors . . . my eyes had never seen such beauty on a plate! It struck me like a cheese knife through the heart—with no fancy occasion in mind, I just had to make a board for myself.

When I was growing up in sunny Southern California, my childhood meals were hearty and casual, with both of my parents sharing the responsibility of cooking for our family of seven. While most meals were served family-style and we hosted numerous events at my parents' home, we never once made a cheese board or charcuterie platter.

My life journeys took me north along the California coast up to the lovely Pacific Northwest, where I have now settled for many years. My husband, Ryan, and I have enjoyed sampling every cuisine the big cities have to offer, from Vietnamese to Thai to Indian to Mexican to . . . (shall I go on?), including many beautifully inspired meals prepared by some of the area's most incredible chefs. I have always been a huge fan of a night out strictly designed around the food. We would bounce around with friends to whatever restaurants or gastropubs were the foodie "must-tries" of the month, laughing and eating our way through the city. These moments defined me. No matter how hard I try not to, I will forever be the girl taking pics of her food and documenting every moment on Instagram!

What started as a promise to myself that I would always try to make my meals beautiful turned into a full-blown obsession with food styling, food photography, and ultimately becoming the woman I want to be. A woman who believes in the power of pretty food and in the power of sharing a gorgeous meal with someone she cares about (or millions on the internet). A woman who believes that what we make and eat can transform us—platters have done that for me. It wasn't until I started focusing on what foods made me feel my best that I discovered I could leave meat out of most of my meals and not miss a bit of food joy. Plus, eating plant-forward cheese boards has helped me lose 115 pounds!

Eating plant-forward just means eating mostly plant-based, choosing foods that are derived from plant sources versus animal sources as often as you can. I believe in following your own intuition when it comes to what you eat and what you feel is healthful and nourishing for you. For me, a limited amount of dairy combined with lots of whole grains and fresh fruits and vegetables has been the ticket to feeling great and full of energy. So here I am, sharing an approach to platters and boards that doesn't rely on salami. I hope it connects with you and gets your mind swirling with even more ideas for cleaner eating and beautiful plates— whether they're designed to elevate any ordinary weeknight or to be shared with guests at a larger gathering.

Put simply, designing platters and boards is taking everyday ingredients and making them fabulous. It's all about allowing your personality, creativity, resourcefulness, and style to shine through in your creation. It's a celebration of food, both in the creative process and in the grazing enjoyment. I can't wait to show you!

XOXO, Lea

Platter Magic

Food can be served in so many ways, but platters make every snack, appetizer, meal, and dessert a true celebration! All the glorious choices are displayed in an artful way to spark conversation and encourage your guests to try new, fun, and unique foods. Plus, when you choose mostly plant-based ingredients, you share healthy habits with friends and family.

But don't save the pretty presentations of boards for only special occasions. Much of your everyday eating can be served in this beautiful way. Fajita Night? Make a platter out of it! Craving dessert? Make a brownie board! Hanging out by the pool? Make grazing baskets! Starting to get the idea? Platters are the new black. And we like black boards too.

It will take you just minutes to assemble healthy, mostly plant-based ingredients into a masterpiece—I believe in you! Tap into your inner designer, crafter, foodie, and shopaholic (maybe that's just me?) to bring together a satisfying array of foods on a gorgeous board.

Ready to get started? You can style a board in so many ways, but I have found some "pillars" of platter making that help you dance through this process. Music encouraged.

CONSIDER A THEME

Are you making a traditional cheese board or using up leftovers from the fridge? Maybe you're designing a specific shape to display or want to feature a special ingredient. Choosing a specific color scheme or going rainbow is an easy way to incorporate a theme with lots of interesting ingredient possibilities that will get your guests talking. The options are practically endless! Planning your board will help you shop, cover any diet-specific needs, and set aside the time to pull it all together.

CHOOSE A PLATTER & DISHES

The size and shape of the board will determine how much food it will hold and how many it will serve. Make sure to choose ramekins and little bowls that balance out the size and shape of the board and also correspond with the number of dips or items in bowls you plan to serve. If you are feeding a larger crowd, you will likely need multiple boards, bowls, and plates filled with different foods to put together more of a grazing spread or grazing table, which is an entire table of food placed directly on a parchment paper–lined tabletop or placed on various pedestals and trays.

While you don't need to have every stylish board and gadget on the market (even though we may want to), it's smart to invest in a few grazing essentials to help ensure a gorgeous end result. Be on the lookout for platter decor that inspires you. I love to discover local, handcrafted items at farmers' markets and shop at antique or thrift stores for vintage plates, linens, and utensils with character. (Just watch that what you use is food-safe or separated from food with a liner.) At the same time, I am not above purchasing items from chain stores, as long as they are made with safe materials and I like the design. You may find:

Wood boards are classic. Yet, at the same time, there has been an explosion of modern styles from incredible local artisans. Wood is great for cutting and serving right on the board, but it also requires special care to maintain its beauty for years to come. If you're a fan of wood boards, pick up a natural board oil and use it generously. Never let your wood boards soak in water. Gently clean them with warm soapy water, dry immediately, then apply oil as needed. I like to let my oil soak in overnight, then wipe off any extra the next day.

Style point: White cheeses, dips, and dishes look amazing on darker wood while vibrant fruits and darker-colored nuts display well on a lighter-colored wood.

Natural stone platters are naturally cold—amazing for serving food that you want to keep chilled in warmer months. Marble is a classic and clean choice that comes in tons of beautiful styles.

Decorative trays and baskets can lend a unique style. I like to use galvanized tin trays. Remember to lay a piece of parchment paper down first to keep the surface food-safe.

Interesting platter shapes inspire and challenge. Don't restrict yourself to one specific shape, especially when there are so many gorgeous styles out there. Right now, you may be into small round boards, but in six months it could be all about the ovals. Allow your platter and board collection to mature and change over time.

Unconventional boards remind us not to take ourselves or our plating too seriously. Look around your house and you will find many different items that could be grounds for grazing. The latest viral trends in charcuterie are centered around creative ideas. The Papayeah Platter on page 46 and Charcuterie Cones on page 105 will give you examples of how to have some fun with display choices. Check out #unconventionalcharcuterie on Instagram for tons of inspiration!

Essential Boarding Accessories

To be party-ready, boards benefit from a few buddies.

Ramekins & bowls. These dishes welcome many types of ingredients, including jams, pickles, olives, dips, and spreads. I love the look of round white ceramic dishes against a dark walnut board or cute glass bowls for displaying pretty green olives. Regardless of what's in the bowl, choosing the right size and shape for your board is essential.

Parchment paper. Keep it on hand to line trays and tables.

Food labels. It's nice (sometimes, essential) to know what type of food you are about to enjoy. Choose from styles that include granite and chalkboard varieties and simply skewers with a little paper flag you can write on.

Cheese knives. These are super important for digging into your cheeses, so you'll need a variety of knives or cheese forks to add to your collection. Because mixing knives is sort of a no-no when it comes to cheeses, pick up a pack of knives with a variety of styles for each cheese type.

Tongs & other serving tools. Provide little tongs and serving spoons or utensils for your guests to grab and serve themselves from your board. I pick up packs of disposable or bamboo varieties at my local party store.

Small plates & napkins. In all the designing excitement, don't forget to place these basics next to your graze.

PLAN YOUR INGREDIENTS

Once you choose your theme and board and assess how many guests you are feeding, you are ready to select and source your ingredients. Where to start? Anywhere! Boards include foods from practically every aisle of the grocery store and every cuisine known to man. Traditional plant-forward (mostly plant-based) boards usually include an array of cheeses, dips and spreads, briny olives and tangy pickles, crackers and breads, seasonal fruits and vegetables, dried fruits and nuts, treats like cookies and chocolate, and pretty herbs and edible flowers as garnish. Feel free to make a list, but leave a little room for sudden inspiration as well. In this book, we will make platters using a variety of ingredients from multiple cuisines and including both ready-to-munch and cooked elements. We will make cheese plates, salad spreads, deconstructed dinners, even dessert boards too. You'll learn how to craft nearly 50 planned boards, but you'll also get random bursts of brilliant board ideas all your own once you catch on! Always feel free to make substitutions based on your personal preferences and availability of selections. Can't find that cranberry honey? Choose any type of honey you enjoy and can find easily.

You will begin to see that having a well-stocked fridge and pantry will allow you to make a beautiful platter almost on the fly. You'll get a sense of what you like to include on boards and can buy any shelf-stable or longer-lasting refrigerated items in bulk. Following is a list of basic ingredients I like to have on hand. Choose vegan varieties in whatever categories you desire.

Cheeses: aged white cheddar, aged Gouda, Brie wheel, plain or honey goat cheese, dill Havarti, some kind of spicy cheese, like a Sicilian Jack

Dips, spreads, and "dishables": marionberry jam, honeys, hummus, spreadable cheeses, ranch dressing, pesto, hot sauce, tzatziki, green olives, cornichons

Fruits: strawberries, grapes, oranges, apples, avocados

Vegetables: cucumbers, baby carrots, grape tomatoes

Pantry items: crackers, nuts, dried fruits, pretzels, cookies, chocolate bars

As much as you can, curate seasonally available produce and other gourmet products to help your local economy and get the freshest ingredients at the height of their flavor. Your best boarding partners will be farm stands and markets that consistently provide quality ingredients you can trust. I am a huge supporter of using what you have access to without guilt or shame. If you can source high-end ingredients, do so. If not, use what you have and make it fabulous!

Serving Size Math

Here is a simple way to remember your serving sizes as easy as 1-2-3 . . . 4-5!

Appetizer Serving:
1 tablespoon of jam or jelly or dip + 1 tablespoon of nuts

2 ounces of cheese + 2 ounces of plant-based meats or salamis

3 ounces of fruits + 3 ounces of vegetables

4 crackers + 4 pieces of bread

5 pieces of dried fruit or chocolate

Dinner Serving:
Double the above serving sizes.

MAKE THE MAGIC HAPPEN

Because placing lots of ingredients can seem overwhelming at first, I like to use what I call the Eat Beautifully method. It's a simple five-step process that helps me stack my ingredients so the end result is gorgeous every time. It works best with traditional cheese boards and charcuterie-type platters, so give yourself some flexibility when working with a zanier spread of ingredients or presentation.

To follow the Eat Beautifully method, prep your ingredients and place them on your platter in this order to achieve a pretty, balanced look:

1. Cheeses (or other main ingredient)

2. Dishes

3. Fruits & veggies

4. Pantry items

5. Garnish

Then stand back and take a pic!

Flex Your Styling

My Eat Beautifully method originally included a step for styling meats, but I have since adopted a mostly plant-based lifestyle and have adjusted it to reflect how to build mostly vegetarian platters. Feel free to use meat options as your third step after placing your cheese and dishes if you choose to use them.

For any platters in this book that are more of a "meal" board containing cooked ingredients, we will break with the usual order and assemble them in a way that works for their unique needs.

1. Cheeses (or Main Ingredients)

The cheeses or main ingredients (for example, wraps on the board on page 98) are the foundation—regardless of whether you are styling a small plate or a large grazing table.

We will cut and style cheeses in multiple ways to keep the platters balanced and interesting, and will use a variety of foods as our main ingredients. When it comes to clean eating, cheeses can be confusing for some. Cheese is a food that is processed, but it's a good, natural process—much like the way wheat is turned into flour for bread. (We like bread too!)

TYPES OF CHEESES:

- **Semisoft** (partially soft skin with a buttery smooth flavor): Colby-Jack, Havarti, Fontina

- **Soft-ripened** (thin skin with a creamy soft center): Brie, Camembert, feta

- **Semihard** (dense texture with strong flavor): cheddar, provolone, Gouda, Monterey Jack

- **Hard** (firm and crumbly texture; strong, salty, and nutty flavor): Parmesan, Gruyère, Asiago, Romano

- **Plant-based or vegan** (no dairy or animal products): cashew cheese, tofu-based cheese, coconut/nutritional yeast–based cheeses

- **Fresh** (no aging required, these cheeses are ready to be devoured as soon as they are made): ricotta, mozzarella, goat cheese

- **Washed-rind** (often with pinkish-orange rinds from being washed with flavored liquids like brandy or salt water and with varying textures): Muenster, Limburger

- **Blue** (delicious caverns of mold give blue varieties their signature color; soft or firm texture with a highly pungent flavor): blue, Gorgonzola, Stilton

Prep Made Easy

You don't need anything too fancy to make your final creation look gorgeous, but having some key kitchen tools on hand is super helpful.

- Large cutting board
- Chef's knife
- Paring knife
- Kitchen shears
- Measuring spoons and cups
- Blender or food processor
- Cheese storage bags or containers to store your cheese (optional)
- Food preparation gloves (optional; I love the black nitrile food-safe ones I find at my local restaurant-supply store)
- Cleaning/antibacterial wipes for quick spills
- Kitchen towels (helps with styling too)
- Paper towels
- Colander for draining rinsed fruits and vegetables

For preparing cooked platters:

- Baking sheet
- Baking dish
- Cast-iron skillet
- Frying pan
- Parchment paper or nonslip baking mat
- Wooden spoons
- Rubber spatulas
- Glass bowls

2. Dishes

Little bowls and ramekins are essential parts of your grazing board, and placing them in an aesthetically pleasing and functional way is important. Consider the size and shape, color, and texture in order to choose the correct dishes for the platter you are using. Choosing a bowl that is too big will dwarf a smaller board, while ramekins that are too small will throw off the balance and not allow for an abundant look. Choose the color and material of your ramekins in contrast to the color and material of your board or platter. Visual interest is created through combining opposites.

What goes in the dishes? Jelly, honey, jams, spreadable cheeses, hummus, olives, green olives, spicy pickles . . . the list goes on, as you'll discover when you dive into the board designs throughout the book!

3. Fruits & Veggies

The abundant variety of produce out there is overwhelming—in a good way! I love to shop with my eyes (and tummy) and choose colorful fruits and veggies planned around my board theme or season. Seasonal and local is always best. Let the chart on the next page give you a quick overview of what's in season and when.

Traditional cheese boards served a small array of fruits (typically grapes, figs, and perhaps some dried fruits), but nowadays the term *grazing* has opened an array of ideas for what can be used on a board. Cut and styled fruits and vegetables can really make a board a showstopper! Highlight each piece's natural beauty by presenting it in a lovely way that will encourage clean eating and hopefully conversation ("Lea, what is *that* called?!"). I find that the more I include healthy, clean fruits and veggies in a spread, the more I eat

Season	Fruits		Veggies	
Winter	• apples • citrus	• pomegranates • grapefruit	• carrots • cauliflower	• potatoes
Spring	• strawberries • apricots • honeydew melon • limes	• mangoes • gooseberries • avocados	• cucumbers • spring greens • spinach • asparagus	• peas • cabbage • lettuce
Summer	• raspberries • blueberries • cherries • plums • strawberries	• tomatoes • watermelon • grapes • kiwis • peaches	• radishes • snap peas • green onions	• eggplant • bell peppers • summer squash
Fall	• apples • blackberries • elderberries	• pears • plums	• mushrooms • pumpkins	• squashes
Year-round	• bananas • papayas • avocados • apples	• grapes • kiwis • oranges • melons	• arugula • beets	• most herbs • carrots

them. Displaying and preparing them in a way that is fresh, tasty, and gorgeous is what it's all about.

Worried about selecting the best fruit? A simple guide is to remember the easy acronym CAT, which stands for Color, Appearance, and Texture.

• **Color:** Fruits and vegetables naturally range in color corresponding to their ripeness. When it comes to fruits, typically the more green or less vibrant in outer skin color, the less ripe it is. The brighter or more intense the color, the more ripe it is.

• **Appearance:** Are there any major discolorations, dents, cuts, or wounds on the outer flesh? Avoid any produce with broken skin. When it comes to styling boards, you want to choose the prettiest. Save the misfits for enjoying on the side.

• **Texture:** Give it a little squeeze with your whole hand rather than just a couple of fingers. This will give you a better picture of the overall texture of your fruit.

A FEW FRUIT TRICKS:

• Try to pull a leaf off a pineapple at the store—if it gives easily, it's ready to take home.

• For avocados, a pricey piece of fruit that you don't want to waste, you can simply do the stump test. Make sure the stump is still intact when you purchase your avocado at the store. When you get home, you can wiggle the stump. If it falls off easily, the avocado is ready to go!

Make the Cut

You can make fruit look extra fancy with a few simple techniques.

To cut guava and kiwi beautifully, carve in a zigzag fashion around the fruit, making sure to cut to the center. Then gently pull the halves apart. You can see the results in Papayeah Platter (page 46) and Friends & Family Circle (page 110).

To score a mango, hold the fruit with the stem pointing up. Cut around the seed, just off-center on both sides to create two "halves." Using a paring knife, cut through the fruit down to the rind but not all the way through to create small squares in the mango flesh. From the rind side, pop the mango flesh outward to show off your creation. You can see the results in Papayeah Platter (page 46). You can find lots of online videos that show the steps in action.

4. Pantry Items

The pantry is where it's at when it's time to party. In this step, we place all the snacks and dried goods, like nuts, crackers, and dried fruit, but also pretty cookies, peach rings or other fun gummy candies, and chocolate. Have fun matching your pantry items to the color scheme or theme—get creative. Nuts and dried fruits are great for filling in little cracks (no one likes to see gaps on a board, just saying), and colorful dried fruits like apricots and cherries or mango and tangerines can really jazz up a bunch of white cheeses. Get fancy with beautiful and tasty French macarons or specialty cookies from your favorite local bakery. I love supporting other creative foodies, and there are tons in the baking industry for you to team up with to create some gorgeous platters.

5. Garnish

I love to use pretty herbs and nontoxic or edible flowers to decorate my final platter whenever I have access to them. Be careful and speak with a florist or gardener about the right choices for serving with food. Ensuring no pesticides or other harmful chemicals are passed on to your platters is key. I like to grow my own fresh herbs at home, where I can control what is used on them. You can also turn to a local farm you trust for beautiful and safe blooms. My favorite herbs to garnish with are basil, rosemary, thyme, and sage. My favorite flowers to use are chamomile, carnations, geraniums, and chrysanthemums. Sometimes daisies and roses call out to me too.

I hope you find my method helpful, but don't feel tied to five steps or any kind of "rules." The most important thing to remember is that building a beautiful platter is all about being in the moment. Don't get too caught up with trying to make a board "perfect"! There isn't really a right or wrong way to create a board. Each board is unique—even the versions you will create from the designs in this book. I only want you to feel inspired to plan and shop for gorgeous platters that are a wonderful addition to your weekly meals with your family and bigger gatherings as well.

Enjoy all that you discover in the following pages. But swap in, swap out, and do what works best for you and others who will share your boards and platters. My ultimate goal is always for you to make your platters your own while seeing the beauty in food!

Anytime

Everyday Royalty	26		Sweet Hot Honey	45
Swirl Girl	29		Papayeah Platter	46
Big Softy	30		Date Night In	49
Pretty in Parmesan	33		Sunday Best	50
Always Hummus	34		DIY Crostini	53
Gouda for You	37		Crabby but Cute	54
Crudités Canvas	38		Takeout Snack Baskets	57
Manchego River	41		New Classic Cheese Balls	58
Caprese Dream	42		Cookie Cutie	61

Grazing

Everyday Royalty

SERVES 4–6 | USES 12" ROUND PLATTER

This simple platter is the perfect welcome to the world of grazing. Keep a selection of flavorful cheeses and pantry powerhouses (like dried apricots and Marcona almonds) on hand, and you can easily put together a luxurious plate that will make you feel like a total queen or king *anytime*. You deserve it!

1 (4-ounce) wedge cave-aged blue cheese, cut in half horizontally

4 ounces smoked cheddar, thinly sliced

4 ounces plain hummus

4 ounces hot pepper jelly (I recommend Kelly's Marionberry Habanero Jelly)

3 ounces whole green Castelvetrano olives

1 (2-ounce) jar cranberry honey

1 English cucumber, sliced

1 cup blackberries

1 cup red cherries

½ cup dried cranberries

½ cup dried apricots

½ cup truffle Marcona almonds

¼ cup sliced dried figs

Parmesan crisps

Italian breadsticks (store-bought or recipe on page 128)

Fresh sage leaves, for garnish

Tomatoes on the vine, for garnish

Olive oil, for garnish

Water crackers

1. Put the blue cheese sections and cheddar slices on the platter.

2. Fill small bowls with the hummus, hot pepper jelly, and olives; place on the platter or just off to the side. Set the cranberry honey on the platter.

3. Place the cucumber slices, blackberries, and cherries.

4. Fill in the gaps with the dried cranberries, dried apricots, Marcona almonds, and dried figs.

5. Tuck in a few Parmesan crisps and Italian breadsticks.

6. Garnish with fresh sage leaves and tomatoes, and swirl the hummus with olive oil (see tip below). Serve with additional Parmesan crisps, Italian breadsticks, and water crackers.

Style Points

Swirl that hummus. Once you've put your creamy hummus into a bowl, don't forget to dress it up. With the back of a spoon, push the surface of the hummus into a swirl shape while holding the bowl secure with your other hand. Garnish with artisan olive oil, salts and herbs, or edible flowers. Instant style.

Swirl Girl

Healthy snacking doesn't need to be boring! This grazing creation is a gift of color, crunch, and plant-forward flavor. Try making your own beet hummus at home (see my easy recipe on page 143), or feel free to purchase a delicious store-bought variety. Don't forget to treat your hummus to a sassy swirl (the simple method is on page 26).

1 cup beet hummus

12 sprouted wheat crackers

8–10 dried mango slices

6 red endive leaves, trimmed

5 baby carrots, sliced in half lengthwise

3 mini sweet peppers, sliced in half lengthwise

2 red radishes, thinly sliced

1 cup blackberries

½ cup blueberries

10 rosemary flatbread crackers

12 dried coconut strips

4–6 dried apricots

3 sweetened dried oranges, sliced in half (see recipe on page 147)

4 Medjool date bars

½ cup coconut cashews

Edible flowers (such as chamomile or geranium), for garnish

Fresh basil leaves, for garnish

Fresh rosemary sprigs, for garnish

1. Fill a small bowl with the hummus; place in the center of the platter.

2. Put the sprouted wheat crackers in a small bowl; place next to the hummus.

3. Make a rose with the dried mango slices (see directions below); place it on the platter.

4. Add the endive, carrots, peppers, radishes, blackberries, and blueberries.

5. Fill in the gaps with the rosemary crackers, coconut strips, dried apricots, dried oranges, Medjool date bars, and coconut cashews.

6. Swirl the hummus (see tip on page 26). Garnish the platter with the flowers, basil, and rosemary.

Style Points

Make a mango rose. Take one slice of dried mango (the thinner the better) and roll it up from one end into a little spiral. Wrap another slice of dried mango around the spiral you just made; continue wrapping until you have used 8 to 10 slices, or the rose looks full. Place the rose into a 2-ounce plastic cup or secure with a wooden pick.

Big Softy

SERVES 6–8 | USES 10 X 21½" OVAL BOARD

One of the most amazing grazing combinations: a creamy smear of soft cheese on a crisp cracker. Top that with a dab of honey and it's taste heaven. Try piling a bit of the vegan chive cashew cheese on a crostini with a touch of lemon honey. Or pile a pita cracker with blue cheese, a blackberry, and a smear of fruit spread for a deliciously unexpected combination of flavors. Take your pick of the platter or sample all the possibilities!

6½ ounces vegan chive cashew cheese

1 (4½-ounce) wedge cave-aged blue cheese, cut in half horizontally

4 ounces goat cheese with chocolate chips or cranberries

4 ounces medium cheddar, thinly sliced

7 garlic-stuffed green olives

3 ounces raspberry-marionberry or raspberry fruit spread

1 (2-ounce) jar Meyer lemon honey

2 clementines, sectioned

1 Granny Smith apple, thinly sliced and spritzed with lemon juice to prevent browning

¾ cup blackberries

3–4 Medjool dates, sliced in half

12 dried tangerines

10 crostini

6–8 pita crackers

½ cup dill pickle almonds

¼ cup mixed nuts

¼ cup coconut cashews

¼ cup shelled pistachios

Fresh basil leaves, for garnish

Fresh mint leaves, for garnish

1. Place the chive cheese, blue cheese, goat cheese, and cheddar on the board.

2. Fill ramekins with the olives and fruit spread. Place them on the board along with the honey jar.

3. Add the clementines, apples, and blackberries.

4. Fill in the gaps with the dates, dried tangerines, crostini, crackers, almonds, mixed nuts, cashews, and pistachios.

5. Garnish with fresh basil and mint leaves. Add a dipper to the honey, if desired.

Taste Tip
Kick it up. Try seasoning the crostini with a za'atar spice blend or a medley of dried thyme, sesame seeds, and lemon zest. Serve the spread with your favorite soup for a satisfying meal.

Pretty in Parmesan

SERVES 4–6 | USES 16 X 12" PADDLE BOARD

Every board you create doesn't need to be over-the-top. (I can rein myself in *sometimes*.) Simple can be sensational and satisfying with just the right mix. The hidden highlight of this harmonious board is the homemade crostini you can make ahead.

1 (8-ounce) wedge Parmesan

2 ounces clover honey

1 (2-ounce) jar Mission fig honey

½ cup dried mango slices

½ cup dried apricots

8 crostini (see recipe below)

3 or 4 Medjool dates,
cut into bite-size pieces

¼ cup sweet-and-spicy or
any candied pecans

¼ cup dried cherries

Italian breadsticks (store-bought or
recipe on page 128)

Fresh basil leaves, for garnish

Fresh sage leaves, for garnish

Fresh thyme sprigs, for garnish

Edible flowers (such as chamomile or
geranium), for garnish

1. Place the Parmesan as a wedge, cubes, or a combination on the board.

2. Fill a small bowl with the clover honey. Place the bowl on the board along with the honey jar.

3. Make a mango rose (see page 29 for directions); display on the board or alongside. Add the apricots to the board.

4. Fan out the crostini across the board.

5. Fill in the gaps with the dates, pecans, dried cherries, and Italian breadsticks.

6. Garnish with fresh basil, sage, thyme, and edible flowers.

Taste Tip

Make your own crostini. Preheat the oven to 400°F. Slice a baguette into ¼-inch-thick disks. Rub each slice with a garlic clove, spread with butter, and place on a baking sheet. Top with freshly grated Parmesan and salt and freshly ground black pepper to taste. Bake for 7 minutes, or until lightly browned and the cheese is melted. Serve immediately, or cool and store in an airtight container for up to 3 days. Warm prior to serving.

Always Hummus

SERVES 4–6 | USES 10½ X 25" BOARD

It's always a good time to put out some hummus! Whether plain or seasoned, hummus is an amazing clean dip that plays well with so many platter options—from veggies and cheese to crackers, crostini, and pretzels. Jazz up the top with a beautiful #hummusswirl, a drizzle of olive oil, pretty fresh herbs, green olives, and a sprinkle of seasoning. With vegan and traditional cheese options, this platter will please a range of grazers.

8 ounces vegan Havarti, sliced into rectangles

8 ounces Manchego, sliced into triangles

1 cup plain hummus

1 cup plant-based chipotle almond dip

6 slices homemade crostini (see recipe on page 33)

1 cup marinated green olives

1 cup pistachios, shells on

24 thin pretzel sticks

½ cup rosemary almonds

½ cup Thai curry cashews

6–8 pistachio nut clusters

2 or 3 dried figs, sliced

Olive oil, for garnish

Chili lime seasoning, for garnish

Fresh sage leaves, for garnish

Fresh thyme sprigs, for garnish

1. Fan out the Havarti and Manchego slices on opposite edges of the board.

2. Put the hummus and chipotle almond dip in small bowls and place them near the center of the board. Add a stack of crostini near each.

3. Place the olives and pistachios in bowls at the top and bottom of the board.

4. Fill in the gaps with the pretzel sticks, almonds, cashews, pistachio nut clusters, and dried figs.

5. Swirl the hummus and garnish with olive oil, chili lime seasoning, and a few green olives.

6. Garnish the platter with the fresh sage and thyme.

Gouda for You

Amazing things happen when you bring together one favorite cheese and some flavorful partners—just like you and your crazy friends. For such a small board, you'll be surprised at all the taste possibilities. Try going sweet with a drizzle of vanilla-cinnamon honey, a bit of dried apricots, and Gouda on top of a rosemary cracker, or trend more tangy with a crostini, pickle, and red pepper hummus combo.

5 ounces Gouda

½ cup roasted red pepper hummus

1 (2-ounce) jar vanilla-cinnamon honey

6–8 sweet-and-spicy pickles

8 cucumber slices

1 orange, sliced

6 crostini (store-bought or recipe on page 33)

8–10 rosemary crackers

½ cup dried Turkish apricots

¼ cup sweet-and-spicy pecans

¼ cup pistachios, shells on

¼ cup smoked almonds

1. Place the Gouda on the board. Slice it on the board, leaving about half still intact.

2. Put the hummus in a small bowl and place it on the board along with the honey jar.

3. Add the pickles, cucumbers, and orange slices in stylish rows.

4. Tuck in the crostini and crackers.

5. Fill in the gaps with the dried apricots, pecans, pistachios, and almonds.

Crudités Canvas

Unexpected veggies like asparagus, radish, and red endive paired with soft, creamy vegan cheese and garnished with beautiful herbs make this platter a work of art, or at least Instagram-worthy. Radicchio bowls will become your new favorite way to serve soft cheeses and dips—they're so pretty and easy to make.

1 small head radicchio

6½ ounces French-style cashew cheese

1 cup spring salad mix

4 or 5 scallions, trimmed

1 bunch asparagus, blanched

8 red endive leaves

2 or 3 mini sweet peppers, cut in half

1 or 2 Persian cucumbers, sliced horizontally

8 snap peas, trimmed

12 baby carrots, cut in half

1 English cucumber, sliced into disks

3 radishes, sliced

2–3 tablespoons edamame, shelled and cooked

Microgreens, for garnish

Everything-but-the-bagel seasoning, for garnish

Dried dill, for garnish

Fresh sage leaves, for garnish

Fresh basil leaves, for garnish

1. Reserve 6 radicchio leaves, then make a radicchio bowl with the remaining leaves (see directions below). Place the bowl in the center of the plate and fill with the cheese.

2. Surround the bowl with the spring salad mix.

3. Top the salad mix with the whole and halved vegetables, starting with the largest and working smaller and smaller.

4. Fill in the gaps with the English cucumber and radish slices and the edamame.

5. Garnish the cheese bowl with a pinch of microgreens, everything-but-the-bagel seasoning, and dried dill. Garnish the plate with fresh sage and basil leaves.

Style Points

Make a radicchio bowl. Remove any outer leaves that are browned or wilted from the radicchio head. Cut just above the stem so that you can pull off the leaves easily. Remove 3 or 4 leaves and stack to form a round bowl. Ready for filling!

Manchego River

SERVES 4–6 | USES 13" ROUND PLATTER

Immerse yourself in a flavor experience as you float down a Manchego river. Manchego is a delicious Spanish cheese made from sheep's milk, which is easier to digest than cow's milk. The nutty, salty flavor is perfect for pairing with sweet honeys and jam, or it can easily go savory paired with a crunchy cornichon. Vegan cheddar offers a great taste experience for those eating strictly plant-based. Whichever you choose, just jump in!

8 ounces Manchego, sliced into triangles

8 ounces vegan white cheddar, sliced

3 ounces ranch dressing

12 cornichons

1 (2-ounce) jar Mission fig honey

1 medium avocado, peeled, sliced, and spritzed with lemon or lime juice to prevent browning

10–12 water crackers

1 small bunch green grapes

3 or 4 mini sweet peppers

¼ cup blueberries

6–8 blackberries

8–10 dried apricots

2 or 3 dried figs, sliced

¼ cup sweet-and-spicy pecans

½ cup pistachios, shells on

Fresh rosemary sprigs, for garnish

Fresh basil leaves, for garnish

Edible flowers (such as chamomile or marigolds), for garnish

1. Place the Manchego triangles down the center of the platter. Fan out the cheddar slices along the outer edges.

2. Put the ranch dressing and cornichons in ramekins; place on the platter along with the jar of honey.

3. Fan out the avocado slices and water crackers.

4. Add the grapes, peppers, blueberries, and blackberries.

5. Fill in the gaps with the dried apricots, dried figs, pecans, and pistachios.

6. Garnish with the rosemary, basil, and edible flowers.

Taste Tip

Expand the bases. Sliced avocado may be an unexpected touch on some platters and boards, but it's a welcome addition for anyone looking for a low-carb alternative to crackers. And it's gluten-free! Always spritz sliced avocado with lemon or lime juice to prevent browning.

Caprese Dream

Travel to the Mediterranean with this delicious array of treats. Pile a toasty crostini high with fresh mozzarella, tomato, and a drizzle of pesto as your starting point, then take the scenic route and explore all the possible pairings. Beyond the ingredients, play up the Italian theme with mostly red, white, and green dishware and napkins.

8 ounces pesto-marinated vegan mozzarella, sliced

8 ounces wine-soaked cheddar, cubed

½ cup pesto

½ cup vegan tzatziki (I recommend Trader Joe's version)

½ cup ranch dressing

2–3 tablespoons whole-grain yellow mustard

½ cup store-bought chickpea masala dip or hummus

1 cup spring salad mix

5–7 herbed crostini (see tip on page 43)

5–7 buttered crostini (store-bought or recipe on page 33)

1 English cucumber, sliced

1 cup green cauliflower, cut into bite-size pieces and blanched

6–8 romaine lettuce hearts, rinsed and sliced in half

10–12 grape tomatoes, halved

3 Roma tomatoes

4 or 5 radishes, sliced

¼ cup Marcona almonds

6–8 green olives

6–8 Italian breadsticks (store-bought or recipe on page 128)

2–3 tablespoons edamame, shelled and cooked

Fresh basil leaves, for garnish

1. Make a mozzarella river down the middle of your board. Add the cheddar near the edges.

2. Put the pesto, tzatziki, ranch dressing, mustard, and chickpea masala dip or hummus in ramekins; arrange on the board.

3. Spread the spring salad mix in a few spots around the board.

4. Fan out the crostini and cucumber slices around the cheese and ramekins.

5. Add the cauliflower, romaine, grape and Roma tomatoes, and radishes.

6. Fill in the gaps with the Marcona almonds and olives.

7. Rest the breadsticks on the pesto ramekin.

8. Garnish with the edamame and fresh basil.

Taste Tip
Customize your crostini. One simple crostini recipe (see page 33) can be adjusted to meet your seasoning needs. For this board, replace the salt and freshly ground black pepper in the basic recipe with a pinch of dried parsley.

Sweet Hot Honey

SERVES 2–4 | USES 15 X 6½" PLATTER

Wake up any ordinary weekday with the flavor combinations that flow from this platter. Use the dried mango as a cracker option for something really delish. It's no wonder that mango is one of the oldest cultivated fruits! It also looks gorgeous on your table when you style it into a rose (see the simple directions on page 29).

1 (8-ounce) log cranberry-cinnamon goat cheese

2–3 tablespoons blackberry jelly

2–3 tablespoons habanero honey

1 navel orange, sliced

10–12 marionberries or blackberries

12–14 slices dried mango, half styled into a mango rose

10–12 dried Turkish apricots

3 or 4 dried Medjool dates, sliced

10–12 pumpkin seed crackers (or sub in your favorite)

Fresh rosemary sprigs, for garnish

Fresh sage leaves, for garnish

Edible flowers (such as chamomile or geranium), for garnish

1. Place the goat cheese log in the center of the platter.

2. Put the jelly and honey into ramekins; place at each end of the platter.

3. Arrange the orange slices, marionberries, dried mango slices, mango rose, dried apricots, and dried dates around the cheese and dishes.

4. Tuck in the crackers.

5. Garnish with the rosemary, sage, and edible flowers.

Papayeah Platter

SERVES 6–8 | USES 12 X 16" TRAY

Papaya is beautiful outside *and* inside. It has a well-deserved rep as a superfruit—filled with heart-healthy and cancer-fighting nutrients and weight-loss benefits. Simply slice papaya in half lengthwise and scoop out the seeds. Then leave the fruit bare and beautiful, or fill it with other fruits like pretty strawberry hearts or Rainier cherries. Either way, it belongs on your boards!

2 cups raspberry Greek-style yogurt

1 (2-ounce) jar Valencia orange honey

3 or 4 mini papayas,
cut in half and seeds removed

2 or 3 pink guavas, carved in halves
(see carving tip on page 21)

2 tropical mangoes, halved and scored
(see scoring tip on page 21)

1 green mango, halved and scored

6–8 strawberries, some whole + some sliced

1 dragon fruit, sliced

6–8 kumquats

2 blood oranges, sliced

1 or 2 limes, sliced

4–6 gooseberries in husk

1–2 teaspoons bee pollen, for garnish

2–3 tablespoons microgreens, for garnish

2 or 3 fresh basil leaves, for garnish

1. Put the yogurt into a small bowl; place in the center of the tray. Put the honey in a ramekin; set in the top corner of the tray.

2. Starting with the largest fruits and working smaller, place them on your tray in an aesthetically pleasing way.

3. Fill in the gaps with the smallest fruits.

4. Garnish with the bee pollen, microgreens, and basil.

Style Points

Get creative. Surprise: Bee pollen makes a fabulous garnish for dips! And hot-pink plastic cafeteria trays deserve a place on your grazing table just as much as acacia boards. Whatever you choose, just keep garnishes edible and serving plates food-safe.

Date Night In

SERVES 2–4 | USES 13" ROUND PLATE

Creamy cheeses are paired with sweet honey to take you from the hectic workweek to cuddle time with *your* honey. Pop on a movie and enjoy a picnic right in your living room, or take your plate out to the backyard for an evening under the stars. Be sure to bring pillows and blankets and perhaps two glasses of a bubbly beverage for a toast.

1 (4-ounce) wedge blue cheese, cut in half horizontally

1 (4-ounce) wedge Gorgonzola, cut in half horizontally

4 ounces Havarti, sliced

1 (2-ounce) jar Mission fig honey

10–12 dried mango slices, some styled into a mango rose

1 orange, sliced then cut in half

½ cup raspberries

1 pear, sliced and arranged in a heart shape

½ cup blackberries

16–18 water crackers

3 or 4 Medjool dates, sliced in half

¼ cup sesame-honey or honey-roasted cashews

¼ cup walnuts

¼ cup dried tangerines

¼ cup dried cranberries

Fresh sage leaves, for garnish

Edible flowers (such as carnations, chamomile, and marigolds), for garnish

1. Place the blue cheese and Gorgonzola wedges and Harvarti slices on the plate.

2. Add the honey jar.

3. Make a mango rose (see page 29 for directions); display on the plate. Add the orange slices, raspberries, pear slices, blackberries, and any remaining mango slices.

4. Fan out some of the water crackers; tuck the remaining crackers under the Havarti slices.

5. Fill in the gaps with the dates, cashews, walnuts, dried tangerines, and dried cranberries.

6. Garnish with fresh sage leaves and edible flowers.

Sunday Best

SERVES 4–6 | USES 8 X 11" TRAY

Farmers' markets and specialty food stores are great places to gather a few more lavish ingredients to try out, like the garlic cheese curds included on this platter. Take a leisurely stroll through all the goodies in store, then get lost in creating a beautiful board. Swirl the sunny lentil hummus and arrange the Gouda triangles in a spiral if you're feeling fancy. Oh and we are, darling, we are!

1 (8-ounce) block balsamic and cipollini onion aged cheddar

4 ounces plain goat cheese

3 ounces garlic cheese curds

3 ounces Gouda, cut into triangles

4 ounces spicy yellow lentil hummus

4 ounces cornichons

3 or 4 mini sweet peppers, sliced in half

2 or 3 radishes, sliced

6 store-bought Parmesan toasts

10–12 sesame crackers

½ cup pistachios, shells on

12 dried apricots

¼ cup dried cranberries

Fresh rosemary sprigs, for garnish

Fresh sage leaves, for garnish

Edible flowers (such as chamomile or geranium), for garnish

1. Place the cheddar, goat cheese, cheese curds, and Gouda triangles on the tray.

2. Put the hummus in a small bowl and set in the center of the tray. Put the cornichons in a small jar and place on the tray.

3. Add the peppers and radishes.

4. Fan out the Parmesan toasts and sesame crackers.

5. Fill in the gaps with the pistachios, dried apricots, and dried cranberries.

6. Swirl the hummus (see page 26 for directions).

7. Garnish with the rosemary, sage, and edible flowers.

DIY Crostini

SERVES 4-6 | USES 12 X 17" BOARD

Everyone loves to make their own unique bite that speaks to their soul. Understated arrangements that help your grazers dig in quickly can be just as welcome as elaborate boards. Enter the DIY crostini. Rely on little bowls to hold your main toppers, so your guests can choose how they'd like to top their bread. Now sit back, relax, and watch the magic unfold!

4 ounces sharp white cheddar, sliced

4 ounces Manchego, sliced into triangles

2 ounces creamy blue cheese spread

3 ounces marinated olive medley

2 ounces black olives, sliced

½ cup halved yellow grape tomatoes

½ cup halved red grape tomatoes marinated with olive oil, salt, and pepper

½ cup sliced green tomatoes marinated with olive oil, salt, and pepper

2 ounces cornichons

2 ounces caramelized onion topping (I recommend Divina or you can make your own)

2–3 tablespoons microgreens

1 (2-ounce jar) balsamic glaze

16–18 crostini (see recipe on page 33)

16–18 Italian breadsticks (store-bought or recipe on page 128)

1 or 2 Cara Cara navel oranges, sliced

½ cup blackberries

Fresh rosemary sprigs, for garnish

1. Fan out the cheddar and Manchego slices near the edges of the board.

2. Put the creamy blue cheese, olive medley, black olives, tomatoes, cornichons, caramelized onions, and microgreens in small bowls. Place on or around the board along with the jar of balsamic glaze.

3. Add the crostini and Italian breadsticks.

4. Spread out the orange slices on the board. Scatter the blackberries. Remove a few accents from the ingredient bowls, and arrange on the board as desired.

5. Garnish with the fresh rosemary.

Taste Tip
Serve salad on the side. Make a simple panzanella salad that pairs perfectly with the crostini offerings. Toss spinach with croutons (store-bought or homemade), tomatoes, onions, Parmesan cheese, and a light dressing of olive oil, vinegar, salt, and pepper.

Crabby but Cute

SERVES 2 | USES 8 X 15" BOARD

Get the little ones in your life excited about grazing and eating healthfully with fun shapes and themes, like this crustacean creation! If the kids join in the styling, keep the focus on the fun, not perfect board placements. Challenge their creativity to see what other edible characters and scenes they can make.

3 ounces vegan garlic-and-herb cheese spread

4 sweetened dried oranges, cut in half (see recipe on page 147)

8 sesame crackers

2 blueberries

½ cup coconut cashews

10 sprouted wheat crackers

12 dried coconut strips

1. Put the cheese spread in a little bowl; place it on the board.

2. Arrange the dried oranges around the bowl, fanning them out to look like crab legs.

3. Fan out the sesame crackers to make the head, then place two blueberries on top to look like eyes.

4. Place two cashews at the bottom of the bowl to look like little crab feet.

5. Arrange the sprouted wheat crackers near the bottom of the board to look like sand.

6. Make a swirl in the spread, just for fancy fun (see directions on page 26).

7. Serve with the rest of the cashews and the coconut strips.

Takeout Snack Baskets

MAKES 3 BASKETS THAT SERVE 2 OR 3 EACH
USES 8" BASKETS LINED WITH PARCHMENT PAPER

These healthy baskets are a great "takeout" option for kids and adults alike—enjoy them poolside or in the backyard. The stuffed peppers are super easy to make and the perfect refuel after a long day of playing Marco Polo or doing yard work. The twisty taralli bring out the fun side of crackers. You'll love the unexpected pop of salty goodness from the dill pickle almonds. Make it an adventure to fill your pantry with fun crackers and nut flavors!

1 cup ranch dressing

1 cup creamy feta dressing

8 ounces aged white cheddar, sliced into rectangles

8 ounces mild cheddar, cubed

10 plant-based stuffed mini peppers (see recipe below)

1 English cucumber, sliced

3 radishes, sliced

1 cup dill pickle almonds

18 fennel taralli

18 flatbread crackers

Fresh basil leaves, for garnish

2 or 3 radishes, with greens on, for garnish

1. Line three plastic baskets with parchment paper.

2. Divide the ranch and feta dressings into three small bowls. (Try a radicchio bowl, directions on page 38, for extra style points!) Place one bowl in the center of each basket and serve the other dressing on the side.

3. Arrange the cheddar cheeses in the baskets.

4. Add the stuffed peppers, cucumber, radish slices, almonds, taralli, and crackers.

5. Garnish with the basil and whole radishes.

Taste Tip
Stuff sweet peppers. Cut five mini sweet peppers in half horizontally, keeping the stem on. Scrape out the seeds, then divide 8 ounces of a tofu-based spread (I recommend Toby's Family Foods) or cream cheese among the pepper halves. Peel and slice one avocado; press an avocado slice on top of each pepper half and spritz with lemon or lime juice. Top with sea salt, red pepper flakes, and dried parsley.

New Classic Cheese Balls

SERVES 4–6 | USES 6½ X 15" TRAY

This old-school appetizer will become a new favorite when you mix in the tang of Gorgonzola and the warmth of pumpkin pie spice. Dress your serving plate with simple but elegant microgreens and serve with rosemary crackers. Add a creamy soup (broccoli-cheddar or butternut squash, anyone?) alongside for a perfect comfort meal.

1 (8-ounce) package vegan cream cheese, softened (I recommend Follow Your Heart)

½ cup Gorgonzola crumbles

½ cup shredded white cheddar

1 tablespoon truffle oil

2 tablespoons pumpkin pie spice, divided

2 tablespoons smoked paprika, divided

½ cup chopped pecans

Microgreens, for garnish

Honey

Rosemary crackers and/or crusty bread

1. In a medium bowl, mix together the cream cheese, Gorgonzola, cheddar, truffle oil, 1 tablespoon of the pumpkin pie spice, and 1 tablespoon of the smoked paprika.

2. Roll the cheese mixture into two large balls. Wrap in plastic wrap and refrigerate for at least 30 minutes.

3. Add the remaining pumpkin pie spice and smoked paprika to a plastic zip-top bag. Remove the cheese balls from the refrigerator and toss them in the bag to coat in the seasoning.

4. Place the chopped pecans in a shallow bowl. Remove the balls from the bag and roll in the chopped pecans.

5. Enjoy immediately or refrigerate in an airtight container for up to 3 days. Serve on a bed of microgreens and paired with honey and rosemary crackers or crusty bread.

Cookie Cutie

Looking to sweeten someone's day? Surprise a special person in your life with a small but tasty token of appreciation. The maple leaf cookies are perfect for the fall season, but you can choose any decorative cookie to pretty up your plate.

4 maple sandwich cookies

8 dried apricots

6–8 dried tangerines

2 honey stroopwafels

6–8 dried apple balls

Edible flowers (such as chamomile), for garnish

Fresh herb sprigs or greenery, for garnish

1. Line the pedestal with parchment paper. Place the maple cookies in a row.

2. Add a row of dried apricots and dried tangerines on each side of the cookies. Place the stroopwafels and tuck in the dried apple balls.

3. Garnish with the edible flowers and fresh herbs or greenery.

Style Points

Can't find dried apple balls? Substitute dried apple dices or slices—just as delicious in a different shape. Make any creative adjustments needed to fit the plate. You are the designer!

Salad

Pretty Little Layers	64		A Pop of Couscous	71
Stars & Cranberries	67		Berries, Balsamic & Butter	72
Happily Avo After	68		Sheet Pan Sensation	75

Spreads

Pretty Little Layers

SERVES 6–8 | USES 5 X 13" SHALLOW BOWL

Tomato, avocado, and feta—oh my! This salad is a delicious and vibrant combo that will get your taste buds excited. The key to a pretty layered salad is to lay down a bed of lettuce, then place your ingredients in rows. It takes a little practice to get everything lined up just right, but it's worth the beautiful results.

DIJON VINAIGRETTE

⅓ cup Dijon mustard

⅓ cup olive oil

2 tablespoons lemon juice

1 clove garlic, minced

2 tablespoons rosemary-infused honey

Salt and freshly ground black pepper
to taste

4 cups spring salad mix

1 tablespoon olive oil

Salt and freshly ground black pepper
to taste

¼ cup pecans

¼ cup shelled salted pistachios

½ cup vegan shredded Parmesan cheese

1 medium avocado, peeled, sliced,
and sprtized with lemon or lime juice
to prevent browning

1 green bell pepper, sliced into strips

12–15 grape tomatoes, halved

4 ounces feta cheese crumbles

Fresh mint leaves, for garnish

1. To prepare the Dijon vinaigrette: In a small bowl, whisk together the Dijon mustard, olive oil, lemon juice, garlic, honey, and salt and pepper. Place in a small bowl to serve or store in an airtight container in the refrigerator for up to 2 weeks.

2. Spread the spring salad mix across the bottom of the bowl; fill the bowl almost to the top, leaving about ¾ to 1 inch of space. Drizzle with the olive oil and sprinkle with the salt and pepper.

3. Place the ingredients on the bowl starting from the top and working in rows: half of the pecans and pistachios, half of the shredded Parmesan cheese, half of the avocado and peppers, half of the grape tomatoes, the feta cheese, the remaining grape tomatoes, the remaining shredded Parmesan cheese, the remaining avocado and peppers, and finally the remaining pecans and pistachios.

4. Garnish with the fresh mint leaves. Serve the vinaigrette on the side.

Stars & Cranberries

SERVES 6–8 | USES 9 X 13" OVAL PLATTER

Goat cheese is designed to be the star, bringing fresh, tangy flavor to this (or any!) bright fruity salad. Not a big fan of goat cheese? Try the flavored versions, like blueberry-vanilla and cranberry-cinnamon, before committing to that stand. To stick with plant-based, go with a vegan cranberry cheese.

BALSAMIC VINAIGRETTE

¼ cup olive oil

¼ cup balsamic vinegar

3 tablespoons cranberry honey

Salt and freshly ground black pepper to taste

3 cups spring salad mix

½ cup blackberries

3 rose apples, 2 thinly sliced + 1 cubed, spritzed with lemon juice to prevent browning

½ cup dried cranberries

10–12 red grapes, halved

½ cup candied pecans (see recipe on page 151)

4 ounces cranberry goat cheese, shaped into stars (see directions below)

1–2 ounces cranberry honey

Fresh basil leaves, for garnish

1. To make the balsamic vinaigrette: In a small bowl, whisk together the olive oil, balsamic vinegar, honey, and salt and pepper.

2. Spread the spring salad mix across the bottom of the platter. Drizzle with the balsamic vinaigrette.

3. Starting from the top, place a row of blackberries followed by the sliced apples, cranberries, grapes, and pecans. Repeat a row of blackberries. Follow with the cubed apples and another row of cranberries, sliced apples, and blackberries. Fill in any gaps with the remaining cranberries.

4. Add the goat cheese stars.

5. Top with a drizzle of cranberry honey. Garnish with the fresh basil.

Style Points

Make cheese stars. In a glass bowl, gently soften 4 ounces of the goat cheese in the microwave for 30 to 60 seconds. Spread the cheese into a thin layer on a cutting board. Use a star-shaped cookie cutter to form stars, then put them on a baking sheet lined with parchment. Pop them into the fridge or freezer for 15 to 20 minutes, or until ready to serve.

Happily Avo After

This bright and light salad platter is filled with the vibrant flavors and colors of avocado, citrus, and blueberries and topped with a classic honey-mustard dressing. Each grazer gets their own baby avocado as a gorgeous, creamy centerpiece for their individual serving plate.

2 cups arugula

1 head butter lettuce, cleaned and trimmed

3 small avocados, peeled, halved, and spritzed with lemon or lime juice to prevent browning

2 navel oranges, peeled and sectioned

1 Fuji apple, sliced and spritzed with lemon juice to prevent browning

4 ounces blueberry-vanilla goat cheese, sliced

½ cup blueberries

¼ cup walnuts

¼ cup chopped dried apricots

4 or 5 Medjool dates, chopped

1–2 tablespoons olive oil

3 tablespoons ghost pepper honey

Juice of 1 lime

Salt and freshly ground black pepper to taste

3 tablespoons chopped fresh cilantro

1½ cups store-bought honey-mustard dressing

1. Spread the arugula and butter lettuce across the bottom of the platter.

2. Top with the avocado halves, orange sections, apple slices, and goat cheese.

3. Fill in the gaps with the blueberries, walnuts, apricots, and dates.

4. Drizzle with the olive oil, ghost pepper honey, and lime juice. Season with salt and pepper.

5. Garnish with the cilantro.

6. Serve with the honey-mustard dressing on the side.

A Pop of Couscous

Couscous comes across like a grain, but it's really just a tiny pasta made from semolina flour and water. The Israeli type is larger than other varieties and can be used in any recipes calling for couscous. You'll love the way it sort of pops in your mouth. Enjoy this satisfying warm salad as part of a larger graze or as the main event for a weeknight dinner.

4 cups baby spinach

1 cup Israeli couscous, cooked according to package instructions

1 or 2 avocados, peeled, sliced, and spritzed with lemon or lime juice to prevent browning

1½ cups butternut squash gnocchi, cooked according to package instructions

½ cup chickpeas, rinsed and drained

½ cup fresh peas

¼ cup chopped pecans

1 teaspoon applewood-smoked sea salt

Chopped fresh cilantro, for garnish

Chopped fresh dill, for garnish

Chopped scallions, for garnish

1. Spread a bed of spinach and couscous across the bottom of the platter.

2. Top with the avocado slices, gnocchi, and chickpeas.

3. Fill in the gaps with the peas and pecans.

4. Garnish with the sea salt, cilantro, dill, and scallions.

Berries, Balsamic & Butter

SERVES 2–4 | USES 9 X 13" OVAL PLATTER

This gorgeous winter salad was inspired by the abundance of fresh blackberries in Oregon every year. Marionberries are the true name of blackberries found only in Marion County, Oregon. But if you can only find standard blackberries, no judgment—they're delicious too! You'll love the sweetness of the honey combined with the fruit and balsamic vinegar dressing.

1 head butter lettuce, rinsed and dried

4 ounces cranberry-cinnamon goat cheese, sliced

1 avocado, peeled, sliced, and spritzed with lemon or lime juice to prevent browning

½ English cucumber, sliced

½ cup blueberries

¼ cup marionberries or blackberries

16–18 red grapes, halved

¼ cup dried figs, sliced

1 shallot, finely chopped

¼ cup chopped fresh cilantro

BALSAMIC VINAIGRETTE

¼ cup balsamic vinegar

2–3 tablespoons olive oil

2–3 tablespoons vanilla-cinnamon honey

1 teaspoon applewood-smoked sea salt

Freshly ground black pepper to taste

1. Spread a bed of butter lettuce across the bottom of the platter.

2. Top with the goat cheese, avocado, and cucumber.

3. Fill in the gaps with the blueberries, marionberries or blackberries, grapes, and dried figs.

4. To make the balsamic vinaigrette: In a small bowl, whisk together the balsamic vinegar, olive oil, honey, and salt and pepper. Drizzle on the salad platter.

5. Garnish with the shallot and cilantro.

Sheet Pan Sensation

SERVES 4–6 | USES 9 X 13" BAKING SHEET

Work your magic to turn a basic sheet pan into a big serving of flavor. The secret ingredient in this salad is the truffle salt, which brings a savory punch of brine. To keep prep simple, make the chickpea salad ahead of time. It's a versatile addition to a ton of menus, plus it's packed with iron, zinc, and antioxidants.

3 cups arugula

1 tablespoon olive oil

1 teaspoon truffle salt

4 ounces dill Havarti, cubed

5 ounces Boursin cheese, crumbled

1 cup chickpea salad (see recipe below)

½ cup cauliflower florets

8 grape tomatoes, halved

1 green bell pepper, diced

2 or 3 radishes, sliced

¼ cup Castelvetrano olives

¼ cup diced celery

Drizzle of balsamic glaze

½ shallot, finely sliced

Fresh basil leaves, for garnish

1. Spread a bed of arugula across the bottom of the baking sheet. Drizzle with the olive oil and sprinkle with the truffle salt.

2. Top with the Havarti, Boursin, chickpea salad, cauliflower, grape tomatoes, bell pepper, radishes, olives, and celery.

3. Drizzle with the balsamic glaze.

4. Garnish with the shallots and fresh basil.

Taste Tip

Add on chickpea salad. This quick salad will find its way onto so many of your platters! Simply combine a 15-ounce can of chickpeas (rinsed and drained), ½ cup halved grape tomatoes, 1 tablespoon finely chopped shallot, and the juice of 1 lemon. Cover and marinate in the refrigerator for at least 1 hour and up to 2 days before serving.

Hot

Roasted Veggie Mezze	78	Sweet, Spicy & Cheesy	90
Fajita Flavor	80	Pita Party	93
Appetizer Pizza	82	Super Sandwiches	94
Brie Mine	85	Grown-Up Grilled Cheese	96
Cheese Battle	86	Crispy Cauliflower Wraps	98
Best Baked Feta	89		

Platters

Roasted Veggie Mezze

SERVES 4–6 | USES 10 X 21½" OVAL BOARD

Roasted vegetables are highly underrated. You can bring out the sweet and tender side of almost any vegetable in just minutes in a high-heat oven. And they look gorgeous on your board! Treat your taste buds to the juxtaposition of warm and cold when you pair the roasted veggies with creamy cheeses and dips.

4½ ounces creamy blue soft-ripened cheese

8 ounces wine-soaked cheddar, sliced into rectangles

1 cup plant-based tofu spread (I recommend Toby's Family Foods Original or Jalapeño Spread)

2 ounces vegan chipotle-almond dip (I recommend Bitchin' Sauce)

1 cup plain hummus

2 ounces garlic hummus

18 green olives

12 sliced sweet pickles

6 peperoncini

1 bunch asparagus, roasted

1 cup broccoli, roasted

3 zucchini, cut into sticks and roasted

1 cup roasted bell peppers

1 sweet onion, sliced and roasted

10–12 grape tomatoes, halved

¼ cup pistachios, shells on

2–3 tablespoons za'atar-based salt, for garnish (I recommend Portland Salt Co)

2 or 3 scallions, trimmed and sliced, for garnish

2 ounces feta cheese crumbles, for garnish

1 French baguette, warmed and sliced

1. Place the creamy blue in the center of the board. Fan out the cheddar slices at each end of the board.

2. Put the tofu spread, chipotle almond dip, plain and garlic hummus, olives, pickles, and peperoncini peppers in small dishes and place on the board.

3. Add the roasted vegetables to the board starting with the asparagus and continuing with the broccoli, zucchini, peppers, and onions.

4. Fill in the gaps with the grape tomatoes and pistachios.

5. Garnish the plain hummus with the za'atar salt, the tofu spread and chipotle dip with the scallions, and the garlic hummus with a few grape tomatoes. Top the asparagus with the feta cheese.

6. Serve immediately with the French baguette slices.

Taste Tip

Roast those veggies. Preheat the oven to 400–425°F. Wash, peel, and trim your vegetables, then slice them into bite-size pieces and toss onto a baking sheet. Coat the veggies evenly with olive oil, salt, and pepper. Add a dash of za'atar seasoning, if you like. Roast in the oven on the center rack for about 25 minutes. It's that simple and delicious.

Fajita Flavor

SERVES 4–6 | USES 12 X 24" RECTANGULAR BOARD

Where's the meat? No one will miss it when you roast delicious vegetables to perfection and set out all the yummy toppings. You can add whatever extra veggies you have in your fridge, but make sure to start with the bell peppers and onion for the best roasted flavor. Serve with refried black beans and stand back while delish taco stacks are created.

**OVEN-ROASTED
FAJITA VEGETABLES**

2 or 3 zucchini, cut into sticks

1 green bell pepper, sliced into strips

1 orange bell pepper, sliced into strips

1 red onion, sliced

2–3 tablespoons olive oil

Salt and freshly ground black pepper to taste

3 tablespoons fajita seasoning (see recipe on page 81)

1 cup shredded Mexican cheese

½ cup crumbled sun-dried tomato feta cheese

½ cup creamy chipotle salsa

¼ cup sour cream

¼ cup guacamole

8–10 grape tomatoes, halved

4 ounces jalapeño potato chips

1 cup sliced Yukon gold potatoes, roasted

8 slices provolone cheese, styled into roses (see page 109 for directions)

12 crispy taco shells

2 Roma tomatoes, sliced

3 or 4 fresh jalapeños, some sliced and some halved

2 or 3 limes, sliced into wedges

¼ cup fresh baby spinach

Fresh cilantro sprigs, for garnish

1 (16-ounce) can refried black beans, warmed

1. To make the fajita vegetables: Preheat the oven to broil. Meanwhile, lay out the zucchini sticks, green and orange bell pepper sticks, and red onion slices on a large baking sheet. Toss with the olive oil, salt, pepper, and fajita seasoning. Roast for 15 minutes, or until the veggies are tender and slightly charred. Toss into a mini cast-iron skillet, and place on the board.

2. Put the shredded Mexican cheese, feta, salsa, sour cream, guacamole, grape tomatoes, potato chips, and roasted potatoes in small dishes; place on the board.

3. Place the provolone roses.

4. Fan out the taco shells and Roma tomato slices.

5. Fill in with the jalapeños, limes, and spinach.

6. Garnish the platter with the fresh cilantro. Place the refried beans in a bowl, top with a sprinkle of the Mexican shredded cheese, and serve on the side.

Taste Tip

Make your own fajita seasoning. Mix 1 tablespoon chili powder, 2 teaspoons cumin, 2 teaspoons onion powder, 1 teaspoon garlic powder, 1 teaspoon smoked paprika, 1 teaspoon regular paprika, 1 teaspoon sugar, 1/2 teaspoon red pepper flakes, and 1/4 teaspoon cayenne.

Appetizer Pizza

SERVES 4–6 | USES 13 X 18" CUTTING BOARD

Pizza makes a perfect appetizer for either family or fancy guests when served on a rustic wooden board! This delicious veggie version features puff pastry topped with a light creamy herb spread and layered with an array of fresh toppings. The recipe idea is super easy to customize with what you have on hand or what your guests will enjoy most. Have fun mixing it up with unique creations.

1 (17.3-ounce) package puff pastry or 2 sheets

10 ounces French garlic-and-fine-herb cheese

Splash of milk or water

3 or 4 fresh basil leaves, finely chopped

Salt and freshly ground black pepper to taste

1 cup bite-size cauliflower pieces

10–12 asparagus spears, cleaned and trimmed

2–3 tablespoons olive oil

1 avocado, peeled, cubed, and spritzed with lemon or lime juice to prevent browning

6–8 grape tomatoes, halved

½ red onion, thinly sliced

4 or 5 black olives, halved

¼ cup shredded Parmesan cheese

2–3 tablespoons thinly sliced scallion

1. Preheat the oven to 375°F, or the temperature indicated on the puff pastry instructions.

2. Spread the pastry onto a baking sheet lined with parchment paper, stretching it to ensure a nice even crust. Bake according to package instructions. Set aside.

3. In a microwavable bowl, soften the French cheese in the microwave for 30 seconds. Mix in a splash of milk or water until a creamy mixture is formed. Add the basil and salt and pepper. Set aside.

4. Preheat the broiler.

5. Toss the cauliflower and asparagus in the olive oil, salt, and pepper. Put together on a baking sheet or on separate sheets. Roast for 10 minutes, then remove the asparagus. Allow the cauliflower to roast an additional 10 to 15 minutes.

6. Spread the French cheese mixture over the cooked pastry as a sauce. Top with the roasted cauliflower and asparagus along with the avocado, grape tomatoes, red onion, black olives, Parmesan cheese, and scallions.

7. Cut into squares to serve.

Brie Mine

SERVES 4–6 | USES 14" ROUND PLATTER

Baked Brie will steal your heart with the first taste. The luscious buttery
goodness never ceases to please, especially when paired with sweet fruits
and a pretty array of nuts, crackers, and lightly toasted crostini.

**1 (8-ounce) wheel Brie,
top cut off with a cheese wire**

¼ cup raspberry-marionberry fruit spread

¼ cup chopped walnuts

**2 rose apples, sliced and spritzed with
lemon juice to prevent browning**

2 navel oranges, sliced

12 rosemary flatbread crackers

**18 crostini (store-bought or
recipe on page 33)**

1 cup pistachios, shells on

¼ cup sweet-and-spicy pecans

Fresh thyme sprigs, for garnish

1. Preheat the oven to 400°F.

2. Put the Brie in an oven-safe dish and top
with the raspberry-marionberry fruit spread
and walnuts. Bake for 15 minutes, or until the
cheese melts. Remove from the oven and let
cool slightly before placing on the platter.

3. Surround the Brie dish with the apples,
oranges, and crackers.

4. Add the crostini and pistachios around
the edge.

5. Fill in the gaps with the pecans.

6. Garnish with the fresh thyme and serve
immediately.

Cheese Battle

SERVES 4–6 | 9 X 13" CERAMIC BAKING DISH

Want to please guests with two styles of eating, or maybe even convince someone to try plant-based? Baked cashew cheese reporting for duty! With goat cheese to back it up, you'll have everyone covered. Paired with delicious roasted chickpeas, cauliflower, and mushrooms, it's a win-win situation on your dish.

6½ ounces vegan cashew cheese

6½ ounces plain goat cheese

2 red radishes, sliced

1 purple radish, sliced

1 cup cauliflower florets

1 cup white mushrooms, sliced

½ cup canned chickpeas, rinsed and drained

6–8 green olives

2–3 tablespoons chopped fresh cilantro

2 teaspoons everything-but-the-bagel seasoning

1–2 tablespoons olive oil

Pinch of red pepper flakes

Salt and freshly ground black pepper to taste

10–12 fruit-and-nut crackers

10–12 Italian breadsticks (store-bought or recipe on page 128)

1. Preheat the oven to 400°F.

2. Place the cashew cheese and goat cheese in a ceramic baking dish. Surround the cheeses with the radishes, cauliflower, mushrooms, chickpeas, olives, and cilantro, keeping the cheeses separated.

3. Top the goat cheese with the everything-but-the-bagel seasoning and the whole dish with the olive oil, red pepper flakes, and salt and pepper.

4. Bake for 15 to 20 minutes, or until the vegetables are soft and slightly browned.

5. Serve with the crackers and breadsticks.

Best Baked Feta

SERVES 4–6 | USES 9 X 13" CERAMIC BAKING DISH

The best platters don't need to be complicated. This recipe is simply delicious and just might be my favorite in the book. Summer is the perfect time to enjoy tomatoes. Their sweetness is unleashed when you roast them and they pair perfectly with tangy feta. Bonus: Your home will be filled with a savory aroma that will call everyone to the grazing table.

1 (7- to 8-ounce) block feta cheese

1 bunch small tomatoes on the vine

12–15 grape tomatoes, halved

1 shallot, thinly sliced

1 or 2 cloves garlic, minced

2 scallions, chopped

2 tablespoons chopped fresh cilantro

2–3 tablespoons olive oil

Crostini (store-bought or recipe on page 33) or flatbread crackers

1. Preheat the oven to 400°F.

2. Put the feta block in the center of a ceramic baking dish. Top and surround with the tomatoes on the vine, grape tomatoes, shallot, garlic, scallions, cilantro, and olive oil.

3. Bake for 15 minutes, or until the tomatoes are slightly browned and wilted.

4. Serve with crostini or flatbread crackers, or set out as a side dish to a larger grazing spread.

Sweet, Spicy & Cheesy

SERVES 4–6 | USES 9 X 13" CERAMIC BAKING DISH

Sound like anyone you know? We all have those sides. We all have a creative side too. This platter was 100 percent inspired by Marissa @thatcheeseplate, who opened me up to the world of cheese plates and unleashed my creative side. Spoon a bit of this dish's comfort onto bread or crackers, or eat straight from the platter (no judgment here!).

4 ounces feta cheese

4 ounces plain goat cheese

6 radishes, thinly sliced

4 mini sweet peppers, sliced

1 shallot, thinly sliced

1 cup bite-size cauliflower pieces

1 cup chickpeas, rinsed, drained, and smashed

½ cup cooked canned collard greens

2–3 tablespoons habanero pepper jelly (I recommend Kelly's Jelly)

1 tablespoon olive oil

Salt and freshly ground black pepper to taste

Crusty bread or crackers

1. Preheat the oven to 400°F.

2. Put the feta and goat cheeses in a ceramic baking dish.

3. Surround the cheeses with the radishes, peppers, shallot, cauliflower, chickpeas, collard greens, and habanero pepper jelly.

4. Top with the olive oil and salt and pepper.

5. Bake for 25 minutes, or until the vegetables are tender and slightly browned.

6. Serve with crusty bread or crackers and additional habanero pepper jelly on the side.

Pita Party

SERVES 4 | USES 18 X 26" BAKING SHEET

Food wrapped in a bread pocket is a simple concept, but the taste when it all comes together is anything but simple. For true pita perfection, give the pockets a few minutes under the broiler after adding your stuffed ingredients. The pockets crisp and the flavors inside find melding magic.

4 whole-wheat pita pockets, cut in half

4 store-bought black bean burger patties

1 cup mushrooms

1 cup fresh or frozen peas, thawed

8 ounces Manchego, sliced

2 ounces creamy feta dressing

8 garlic-stuffed green olives

6 peperoncini

2 tablespoons hot sauce

6 mini sweet peppers, halved

2 cups spring salad mix

2–3 tablespoons microgreens

1 or 2 purple radishes, thinly sliced

2 or 3 rainbow carrots, halved

¼ cup blueberries

8–10 dried apricots

**2 teaspoons steak salt
(I recommend Portland Salt Co)**

Fresh mint leaves, for garnish

Fresh cilantro sprigs, for garnish

1. Cut the pitas in half to create a pocket and warm them in the oven for about 5 to 10 minutes, or until pliable; place on the baking sheet.

2. Prepare the black bean patties according to package instructions; fan out in the center of the baking sheet.

3. Sauté the mushrooms and peas. Put them in a small bowl and place on the baking sheet.

4. Add the Manchego to the baking sheet.

5. Put the feta dressing, olives, peperoncini, and hot sauce into small bowls; add to the baking sheet.

6. Tuck in the mini peppers, spring salad mix, microgreens, radishes, carrots, blueberries, and dried apricots.

7. Sprinkle the patties with the steak salt. Garnish with the fresh mint and cilantro.

Taste Tip
Take back to the oven. Once you and your fellow grazers fill the pitas with fixings, you can eat them immediately or take them back to the oven. For a crispier pita treat, put your creations on a baking sheet, drizzle on a bit of olive oil, and sprinkle with salt, then give them a quick trip under the broiler.

Super Sandwiches

Even if you can't name the players and follow the action, you'll be a fan of these plant-based "chicken" sandwiches. The patties make the perfect little footballs to place inside a soft bolillo roll. Just cut out little strips of vegan cheese and place on top of the chicken patties; melt under the broiler in minutes for a fun and delicious game day.

6 plant-based "chicken" patties

6 bolillo rolls

6 vegan smoked Gouda slices

6 romaine leaves

2 tablespoons vegan mayo

2 tablespoons honey mustard

12 cornichons

1 avocado, peeled, thinly sliced, and spritzed with lemon or lime juice to prevent browning

2 bunches tomatoes on the vine

2 or 3 oranges, peeled and sliced

½ cup pistachios, shells on

1 teaspoon everything-but-the-bagel seasoning

Veggie sticks

1. Prepare the plant-based chicken patties according to package instructions.

2. Preheat the oven to 375°F.

3. Cut the bolillo rolls in half and warm them either on a baking sheet or directly on the oven rack for 5 to 6 minutes, or until soft.

4. While the rolls are warming, slice the Gouda into thin strips (one longer strip and three or four smaller strips, to look like football laces).

5. Place the patties with the cheese styled on top on a baking sheet and melt in the oven.

6. Put two romaine leaves on each roll bottom, then stack a patty on top. Place the sandwiches across the center of the plate.

7. Put the mayo, honey mustard, and cornichons in small dishes; place on or near the plate.

8. Fan out the avocado on the plate. Add the tomatoes on the vine and oranges.

9. Fill in the gaps with the pistachios.

10. Garnish the avocado with the everything-but-the-bagel seasoning.

11. Serve with veggie sticks.

Grown-Up Grilled Cheese

Take your grilled cheese accompaniments way beyond tomato soup! Prepare a pretty relish platter with pickles, pereroncini, olives, marinara and ranch dressing for dipping . . . yesss to all of it. Challenge your household or guests to come up with the most creative and tasty grilled cheese sandwich combos.

RELISH PLATTER

2 ounces feta cheese crumbles

1 cup marinara, warmed

6 tablespoons ranch dressing

18–20 cornichons

8 peperoncini

6 grape tomatoes

6 garlic-stuffed green olives

1 English cucumber, sliced

8–10 fresh green beans, washed and trimmed

2 or 3 radishes, sliced

10–12 mini sweet peppers, half sliced and blackened under the broiler for 5 minutes and half raw

1 avocado, peeled, sliced, and spritzed with lemon or lime juice to prevent browning

1 bunch green grapes

¼ cup salted Marcona almonds

Broccoli microgreens, for garnish

GRILLED CHEESE SANDWICHES

4 tablespoons butter

8 ounces sharp cheddar, sliced into rectangles

4 ounces white cheddar, crumbled

1 cup Romano cheese, grated

8 slices bread of your choice

1. To make the relish platter: Put the feta, marinara, ranch dressing, cornichons, peperoncini, grape tomatoes, olives, cucumber, green beans, and radishes in small dishes; place within the larger oval dish.

2. Fill in the gaps with the mini sweet peppers, avocado, grapes, and almonds. Garnish with the broccoli microgreens.

3. To make the grilled cheese sandwiches: Warm a nonstick skillet over medium heat. Melt ¹/₂ tablespoon of the butter.

4. Meanwhile, layer two slices of sharp cheddar, one-fourth of the crumbled white cheddar, and ¹/₄ cup of the grated Romano cheese on top of one slice of the bread. Top with another slice of bread.

5. Add the sandwich to the pan and move around to coat the bread with the butter. Cook for 4 to 5 minutes or until golden brown. With a large spatula, pick up the sandwich. Add ¹/₂ tablespoon of butter to the skillet to melt. Flip the sandwich back into the pan and cook for 4 to 5 minutes, or until golden brown on the second side.

6. Remove from the heat onto a paper towel–lined plate or cutting board. Cut in half diagonally; keep warm. Repeat to make four sandwiches.

7. Place the sandwich halves on the rectangular platter. Serve with the relish dish.

Crispy Cauliflower Wraps

SERVES 4–6 | USES 13" ROUND PLATTER

These vegan and gluten-free fried cauliflower bites are going to make you ask yourself two questions: Where is the nearest head of cauliflower, and why do I need to eat anything else ever again? Maybe that's a bit extreme, but after trying these wraps I think you'll know what I'm talking about.

2 cups gluten-free flour

2 teaspoons garlic powder

2 teaspoons onion powder

1 teaspoon cayenne pepper

2 teaspoons salt

1 teaspoon freshly ground black pepper

1 cup water

1 head cauliflower, cut into bite-size pieces

2 cups oil, for frying

2 ounces vegan Chao cheese, shredded

½ cup store-bought chipotle almond spread or spicy hummus

½ cup creamy honey mustard

10–12 grape tomatoes, halved

½ cup chopped fresh cilantro

10 beet tortillas, warmed

1 head butter lettuce, cleaned and stem removed

Spicy seasoning mix of your choice, for serving

1. In a large bowl, combine the flour, garlic powder, onion powder, cayenne pepper, salt, and black pepper. Whisk in the water until a batter forms.

2. Add the cauliflower to the batter and toss until evenly coated.

3. Heat the oil in a Dutch oven over medium heat. Carefully add the cauliflower in batches and fry for 4 to 6 minutes, or until golden brown.

4. Drain on a paper towel–lined plate, then transfer to a covered dish to keep warm.

5. Put the shredded cheese, chipotle almond spread, honey mustard, grape tomatoes, and cilantro in small bowls; place on or around the platter.

6. Fan out the tortillas and butter lettuce leaves on the platter.

7. Uncover the crispy cauliflower bites to serve on the side of the platter. Set out the spicy seasoning mix.

Sweets &

Patriotic Platter	102
Charcuterie Cones	105
Eat the Rainbow	106
Grazing Cane	109
Friends & Family Circle	110
Bring It to the Table	113

Crowd-Pleasing Crudités	114
Ready-for-Broadcast Board	116
Hot Cocoa Bomb Board	118
Gifts of Grazing	121
PB & Brownie Party	122
Raspberry (S)tart	125

Celebrations

Patriotic Platter

SERVES 4–6 | USES 11" ROUND PLATTER

Celebrate your independence with red, white, and blue plant-based selections! This platter features some of the most fun board trends: cheese cutouts and an apple heart. Press out festive star shapes with a cookie cutter for adorable additions. Then use the cookie cutter as a container for the blueberries. Adding an apple heart to your platter requires only creative positioning and a little practice.

½ cup blueberries

4 ounces Manchego, sliced into triangles

3 ounces dill Havarti, cubed

8–10 provolone slices, some rolled in swirls and some cut out for stars

2 red apples, sliced and some styled into a heart, spritzed with lemon juice to prevent browning

8 watermelon wedges

1 or 2 small bunches red grapes

½ cup raspberries

½ cup blackberries

½ cup red cherries

6–8 red grape tomatoes, halved

1 cup Chex Mix Muddy Buddies

8 white yogurt-covered pretzels

1. Place the star cookie cutter in the center of the platter. Fill the cookie cutter with blueberries.

2. Place the Manchego, dill Havarti, and provolone swirls.

3. Arrange some of the apple slices in a heart shape. Add the watermelon, grapes, and remaining blueberries and apples.

4. Fill in the gaps with the raspberries, blackberries, cherries, tomatoes, Muddy Buddies mix, and pretzels.

5. Top with the provolone stars.

Charcuterie Cones

SERVES 8 | USES SCRAPBOOK PAPER + CONE HOLDER

Social media can drive culinary creativity. Prime example: charcuterie cones, individual servings of snacking heaven packaged in adorable scrapbook paper. These cones hold a mixture of savory and sweet for the complete package. Feel free to display your own creativity and swap in whatever fits the season, occasion, and grazers. Get hints below for making the cones.

1 cup cashews

16 ounces vegan Chao cheese, cubed

8 green pimento-stuffed olives

8 vegan smoked turkey slices

8 vanilla wafer cookies

16 vegan gummy bears

8 peppermint lollipops

8 candy canes

8 dried lavender stems, for garnish

Edible flowers (such as chrysanthemum), for garnish

1. Place the paper cones in the holder. Line with trimmed parchment paper.

2. Divide the cashews among the cones.

3. On eight wooden skewers, thread four or five cubes of cheese each. Top each with an olive. Add to the cones.

4. Roll the turkey slices and add one to each cone.

5. Into each cone, tuck in a cookie, two gummy bears, a lollipop, and a candy cane.

6. Garnish each cone with a lavender stem and an edible flower.

Style Points

Make a scrapbook-paper cone. Start with a rectangular. Fold the top left corner down to the bottom right corner, creating a triangle. Take the bottom left corner and fold it up to meet the top point of the triangle. Take the bottom right corner and fold it up to meet the top point of the triangle. Then roll into a cone, starting at the lower left and keeping the point tight at the bottom. Secure with double-sided tape.

Eat the Rainbow

SERVES 12 | USES 19" ROUND PADDLE BOARD

Dedicate this delicious rainbow board to the raw foodies in your life. It's half crudités and half *heck yeah*, with a colorful array of fruits and veggies to pair with creamy cheeses. Bonus: bee pollen! It's a crazy-healthy mix of flower pollen, bee secretions, nectar, honey, enzymes, and wax made by worker bees for the hive.

1 (4-ounce) wedge Gorgonzola, cut in half horizontally

4 ounces goat cheese

4 ounces blueberry-vanilla goat cheese

1 (2-ounce) jar Valencia orange honey

1 (2-ounce) jar ghost pepper honey

1 (4-ounce) jar apricot fruit spread

2–3 tablespoons bee pollen granules (I recommend Naturacentric)

8 raw broccolini stalks, trimmed

1 green bell pepper, sliced into strips

1 red bell pepper, sliced in half and displayed with seeds exposed

4 mini orange sweet peppers

2 blood oranges, sliced

1 Cara Cara navel orange, sliced

1 or 2 bunches green grapes

2 Fuji apples, sliced and spritzed with lemon juice to prevent browning

1 Granny Smith apple, sliced and spritzed with lemon juice to prevent browning

16 raw zucchini slices, folded in ribbons

1 English cucumber, sliced

1 mango, sliced

1 mini papaya, sliced in half and displayed with seeds exposed

1 lime, sliced

1 carrot, sliced into rounds

3 Medjool dates, sliced in half

16 dried apricots

Fresh basil leaves, for garnish

Savory rice crackers

1. Place the Gorgonzola and goat cheeses at intervals around the edge of the board.

2. Place the orange honey in its jar or a small dish on the board. Add the jars of ghost pepper honey and apricot fruit spread to the board. Put the bee pollen in a small bowl and add to the board.

3. Place the broccolini, bell peppers, blood oranges, Cara Cara orange, grapes, Fuji apples, Granny Smith apples, zucchini, cucumber, mango, and papaya on the board.

4. Fill in the gaps with the lime, carrot, dates, and dried apricots.

5. Top the plain goat cheese with a drizzle of the orange honey and a sprinkle of the bee pollen granules. Garnish the board with the fresh basil.

6. Serve with savory rice crackers on the side.

Grazing Cane

SERVES 6–8 | USES 24" CERAMIC TILE

Make creativity a gift to your guests! The secret to getting the candy cane just right: lay down a little bed of arugula to give yourself a framework for the shape. Once you get the form you want, top with the main ingredients and garnish your festive creation to the nines.

1 cup arugula

24–30 provolone slices, shaped into 6 roses (see directions below)

4 ounces white cheddar, sliced

4 ounces pepper Jack cheese, sliced

1 apple, sliced and spritzed with lemon juice to prevent browning

8 grape tomatoes, halved

2 Persian cucumbers, sliced

½ cup blackberries

3 or 4 sweetened dried oranges, halved (see recipe on page 147)

¼ cup dried cranberries

6–8 rosemary crackers + more served on the side

6–8 sprouted wheat crackers + more served on the side

Edible flowers (such as chamomile), for garnish

Fresh basil leaves, for garnish

1. Spread a bed of arugula in a candy cane shape on the clean tile surface.

2. Place the provolone roses on the arugula, evenly spread out along the length of the candy cane shape. Add the cheddar and pepper Jack, fanning out the slices.

3. Fill in the gaps with the apple slices, grape tomatoes, cucumbers, blackberries, dried oranges, and dried cranberries.

4. Tuck in a few horizontal stacks of three or four crackers each.

5. Garnish with the edible flowers and basil. Serve with more crackers on the side.

Style Points

Wrap a rose. Salami doesn't have a monopoly on crafted roses for boards. You can make beautiful white ones using dairy or plant-based provolone slices of about 2" diameter. (To trim a larger slice, use a circle-shaped cookie cutter.) On a large flat surface, place a few cheese slices in a long row, layering them so that each slice is covering half of the slice before it. Roll the slices tightly from one side. You can add more slices around the outside to fill out the "petals."

Friends & Family Circle

SERVES 12+ | USES 24" ROUND BOARD

The cheese board is the secret favorite at every gathering! So pack it with pleasers for even the pickiest of eaters and plenty of clean-eating options as well. Yep, there's meat and some dairy cheeses on this platter because we all know Uncle Jim needs his salami with smoked cheddar!

1 loaf Kalamata olive bread, warmed and then sliced

1 French baguette, warmed and then sliced

8 ounces triple crème Brie

8 ounces aged white cheddar, crumbled into bite-size pieces

8 ounces smoked cheddar, sliced into rectangles

4 ounces vegan blue cheese

4 ounces blueberry-vanilla goat cheese

4 ounces plain goat cheese

8 ounces cranberry goat cheese

1 cup tofu-based dip

1 cup tzatziki

1 cup plain hummus

1 (12-ounce) jar marionberry-habanero jelly

1 (2-ounce) jar cranberry honey

8 ounces Italian dry salami, styled into salami roses (see rose directions on page 109)

8 ounces peppered salami, folded and skewered

8 ounces Genoa salami, folded

1 Calabrese salami, sliced

½ cup sliced dill pickles

3 or 4 bunches red grapes

2 or 3 tangelos, halved

1 or 2 Granny Smith apples, sliced, spritzed with lemon juice to prevent browning, and styled into "apple hearts" (see photo)

1 large English cucumber, sliced

5 ounces three-seed beet crackers

½ cup grape tomatoes

½ cup raspberries

½ cup dried tangerines

10 dried mango slices

24 dried apricots

½ cup pistachios, shells on

1 cup cashews

1 cup trail mix

Fresh sage leaves, for garnish

Fresh oregano sprigs, for garnish

Microgreens, for garnish

Edible flowers (such as chamomile, roses, and violas), for garnish

1. Fan out the olive bread slices down the center of the board. Place the baguette slices on each side of the board.

2. Space the Brie, white cheddar, smoked cheddar, blue cheese, and goat cheeses around the board.

3. Put the dips and hummus in small bowls; place on the board. Add the jelly and honey jars.

4. Add the salami roses, salami skewers, salami folds, salami slices, pickles, grapes, tangelos, apples, and cucumber.

5. Tuck in the beet crackers and fill in the gaps with the grape tomatoes, raspberries, dried tangerines, dried mango, dried apricots, pistachios, cashews, and trail mix.

6. Garnish with the sage, oregano, microgreens, and edible flowers.

Bring It to the Table

SERVES 12 | USES 18 X 24" BUTCHER PAPER

This is the straight shooter of grazing displays. No fancy boards or platters required—just butcher paper and your tabletop or countertop. Let the vibrant fruits and vegetables, gorgeous grains, and, of course, the cheeses run the show. Pretty flowers and herbs and your satisfied guests gathered around the table complete the perfect picture.

8 ounces pink cheddar, cut into triangles

8 ounces sage Derby, some sliced

8 ounces Romano, cubed

2 ounces sage-and-walnut honey (I recommend Naturacentric)

1 (2-ounce) jar blackberry mulled merlot jam

1 whole orange

2 oranges, peeled and sectioned

3 whole cherry tomatoes

1 cup dried apricots

1 cup dried tangerines

½ cup dried cranberries

½ cup Marcona almonds

1 (4.25-ounce) package water crackers

10–12 everything-but-the-bagel Parmesan crisps

½ cup peach ring gummies

1 cup deluxe mixed nuts

1 cup double-chocolate trail mix

½ cup candied walnuts

Fresh basil leaves, for garnish

Edible flowers (such as carnations and chamomile), for garnish

1. Place the cheddar, sage Derby, and Romano cheeses on the paper.

2. Put the sage-and-walnut honey into a small bowl and place on the paper along with the jar of jam.

3. Add the oranges, tomatoes, dried apricots, dried tangerines, dried cranberries, and Marcona almonds.

4. Place the water crackers and Parmesan crisps.

5. Fill in the gaps with the peach rings, mixed nuts, and trail mix.

6. Top the honey with the candied walnuts. Garnish the spread with the fresh basil and edible flowers.

Crowd-Pleasing Crudités

SERVES 12 | USES 24" ROUND PADDLE BOARD

You decide what's more beautiful: the bright colors and varied shapes on this board or the fact that it's packed with healthy and delicious choices meant to be shared. Try creating your own gorgeous arrangements—get inspired by checking out #tuesdaycrudesday on Instagram!

8 ounces vegan tzatziki

1 radicchio bowl
(see page 38 for directions)

½ cup ranch dressing

3 ounces spring salad mix

10–12 spears roasted asparagus
(see roasting tip on page 79)

12–14 French green beans

½ head cauliflower, cut into florets

10–12 rainbow carrots, halved

8–10 mini sweet peppers, halved

12 green endive leaves

6 red endive leaves

1 English cucumber, sliced

4–6 radishes, sliced

5 or 6 white mushrooms, sliced

6–8 baby corn cobs, halved

10–12 grape tomatoes, some halved and some whole

3 or 4 scallions, trimmed and halved

¼ cup shelled and cooked edamame

Microgreens, for garnish

Fresh basil leaves, for garnish

Fresh curly parsley, for garnish

1. Put the tzatziki in a radicchio bowl and the ranch dressing in a small ceramic bowl; place them on the board.

2. Spread the spring salad mix in a bed across the bottom of the board and surrounding the dips.

3. Place the longest and bulkiest vegetables first: the asparagus spears, green beans, cauliflower, rainbow carrots, and sweet peppers.

4. Continue to fill in with the smaller vegetables like the endive, cucumber, radishes, mushrooms, baby corn, tomatoes, scallions, and edamame.

5. Garnish with the microgreens, basil, and parsley.

Ready-for-Broadcast Board

SERVES 12 | USES 24" ROUND PADDLE BOARD

I may or may not have made this board for an audition for a major television network—and got the role! This showstopping board will be a major hit in your home at the holidays. The warm and cozy color scheme is full-on fall. Elevate the festive seasonal vibes by serving your dip in a cute little gourd.

1 cup red pepper hummus

1 acorn squash bowl
(see directions on page 117)

8 ounces double crème Brie

4 ounces cave-aged blue cheese

8 ounces Vino Rosso aged white cheddar

4 ounces herbed goat cheese

1 cup plain hummus

3 tablespoons marionberry-habanero jelly

8 blue cheese–stuffed green olives

8 cornichons

1 cup pumpkin-pie almonds
or candied almonds

1 (2-ounce) jar vanilla-cinnamon honey

8 strawberries

1 small bunch red grapes

2 small bunches purple grapes

1 cucumber, sliced

1 or 2 kiwi, carved in halves
(see carving tip on page 21)

6 whole mini sweet peppers

8 cherry tomatoes, some whole
+ some halved

2 clementines, whole

1 pomegranate, sliced in half

18–20 fruit and nut crackers

6 buttered toast crackers

16 mini pumpkin spice yogurt-covered
pretzels

½ cup chili mango peach ring gummies

6 pumpkin spice sandwich cookies

12 dried apricots

2 or 3 dried figs, sliced

Fresh sage leaves, for garnish

Edible flowers (such as chamomile),
for garnish

1. Put the red pepper hummus in the acorn squash bowl; place in the center of the board.

2. Place the Brie, blue cheese, cheddar, and goat cheese on the board.

3. Put the plain hummus, jelly, olives, cornichons, and pumpkin-pie almonds or candied almonds in small bowls; place on the board. Add the honey jar.

4. Add the strawberries, grapes, cucumber, kiwi, peppers, tomatoes, clementines, pomegranate, crackers, pretzels, gummies, and cookies, looking for ways to make color pop all around the board.

5. Fill in the gaps with the dried apricots and figs.

6. Garnish with the fresh sage and edible flowers.

Style Points

Make an acorn squash bowl. Cut the top off an acorn squash (about $3/4$ inch from the stem) and scoop out the seeds. If the squash will not stand upright, slice the bottom slightly to create a flat surface. Fill with dip and display the "lid" (top) off to the side of the bowl.

Hot Cocoa Bomb Board

SERVES 8 | USES 19" ROUND PADDLE BOARD

Hot cocoa bombs will be the hit of the party! Get some milk warming on the stove or in a slow cooker and set out festive mugs. Pour the milk, then let your guests drop their bombs and choose their favorite hot cocoa toppings and pairings. The ingredient list here has tons of ideas, but you can customize your board with whatever treats will get your guests smiling and reminiscing about holiday memories.

8 milk chocolate hot cocoa bombs

½ cup crushed peppermints

2 cups mini marshmallows

2–3 dozen assorted sugar cookies

8 dark chocolate peppermint sandwich cookies

8 peppermint toffee candies

8 mini brownies

8 large yogurt-covered pretzels

8 dark chocolate truffles

8 candy canes

8 ounces mixed fruit gumdrops

8 strawberry gummy lips

1 dark chocolate bar, broken into small pieces

Carrot fronds, for garnish

Edible flowers (such as chamomile), for garnish

1. Put the hot cocoa bombs, crushed peppermints, and 1½ cups of the marshmallows in small bowls and place on the board.

2. Place the larger treats: sugar cookies, sandwich cookies, toffee candies, and brownies.

3. Tuck in the pretzels, truffles, and candy canes.

4. Fill in the gaps with the gumdrops, gummy lips, dark chocolate pieces, and the remaining mini marshmallows.

5. Garnish with the carrot fronds and edible flowers.

Gifts of Grazing

SERVES 2-4
USES 12 X 16" RECTANGULAR BOARD + 16" ROUND SLATE BOARD

Unconventional charcuterie is a term used in the grazing community to describe unusual ways to serve charcuterie or out-of-the-box designs. This holiday gift presentation is exactly that! Have fun finding hilarious stocking stuffers to spruce up your platter, like this "boyfriend" chocolate candy. Cheese plates don't always need to be taken so seriously.

4 ounces dill Havarti, sliced into long rectangles

Fresh rosemary sprigs (go long!), plus more for garnish

4 ounces creamy Havarti, cubed

4 ounces Manchego, sliced into triangles

1 Gala apple, sliced and spritzed with lemon juice to prevent browning

6 strawberries, halved with stems on

6–8 grape tomatoes, halved

4 sweetened dried oranges, cut in half or quarters (see recipe on page 147)

6–8 fruit and nut crackers + more for serving on the side

6 mini peanut butter cups

3 dried Medjool dates, quartered

¼ cup Marcona almonds

Fresh sage leaves, for garnish

Fresh oregano sprigs, for garnish

Edible flowers, for garnish

1. Place enough dill Havarti across the round board to create a "ribbon." Create a ribbon across the rectangular board with the long sprigs of rosemary.

2. Add the creamy Havarti, Manchego, apple, strawberries, tomatoes, dried oranges, crackers, and peanut butter cups to the board.

3. Fill in the gaps with the dates and almonds.

4. Garnish with the rosemary, sage, oregano, and edible flowers.

5. Use a fun stocking stuffer (edible is best) for the centerpiece of each board.

PB & Brownie Party

SERVES 6–8 | USES 13" ROUND PEDESTAL

There's no shame in going the semi-homemade route to get the party started more quickly! Pair brownies made from a mix with a simple homemade peanut butter frosting that you may just find yourself featuring on all kinds of boards. The special finishing touch: strawberry hearts—an easy food styling trick that takes no time at all.

1 (18-ounce) package brownie mix

1 cup peanut butter frosting (see recipe on page 152)

2 teaspoons + 2 tablespoons sea salt, divided

2 tablespoons raspberry-marionberry fruit spread

6–8 strawberries, cut into hearts (see directions below)

4 dried Medjool dates, chopped

¼ cup dried tangerines

¼ cup candied walnuts

2–3 tablespoons cinnamon sugar, for sprinkling

1 navel orange, sliced

¼ cup Marcona almonds

Fresh rosemary sprigs, for garnish

Edible flowers (such as chamomile), for garnish

1. Prepare the brownies according to package instructions.

2. Meanwhile, prepare the peanut butter frosting and set aside.

3. Remove the brownies from the oven and sprinkle with the 2 teaspoons of sea salt. Let them cool for about 15 minutes before cutting.

4. Cut the cooled brownies into squares and place them in a stack on the pedestal.

5. Put the frosting, remaining sea salt, raspberry-marionberry fruit spread, strawberry hearts, dates, tangerines, walnuts, and cinnamon sugar in small dishes; add to the pedestal and around it.

6. Tuck in the orange slices around the board and fill in the gaps with the almonds.

7. Garnish with the fresh rosemary and edible flowers.

Style Points

Cut a strawberry heart. Simply slice off the top of a strawberry in a V-shape. Then cut the strawberry vertically from top to bottom to create two hearts.

Raspberry (S)tart

SERVES 6–8 | USES 9 X 13" OVAL PLATTER

Need an attention-grabbing centerpiece for a dessert or fruit board? This gorgeous tart is a sweet starter that comes together in a flash! It features a simple prepared pie crust dressed with a light and slightly spicy strawberry-habanero mascarpone cream and a delish raspberry topping. It's perfect for summer celebrations or simply backyard chilling and grazing.

1 (11-ounce) pie crust

16 ounces mascarpone cheese

¾ cup strawberry-habanero jelly, divided (I recommend Kelly's Jelly)

2 cups raspberries, divided

2 tablespoons sugar

Squeeze of lemon juice

Drizzle of rosemary-infused honey (I like Naturacentric)

Fresh mint leaves, for garnish

1. Preheat the oven to 350°F, or the temperature indicated on the pie crust instructions.

2. Spread the crust into a ceramic oval baking dish. Bake according to package instructions. Set aside to cool.

3. In a medium bowl, whip the mascarpone until creamy. Gently fold in ½ cup of the strawberry-habanero jelly. Set aside.

4. Combine 1½ cups of the raspberries, sugar, and lemon juice in a saucepan over medium heat. Cook and stir until the raspberries break down and the sugar dissolves, about 3 to 5 minutes. Remove the raspberry mixture from the heat and add the remaining ¼ cup of strawberry-habanero jelly.

5. To assemble the tart, place the crust on a platter. Top the crust with the whipped mascarpone, making sure the top looks smooth with some gentle peaks. Follow with the raspberry mixture and the remaining ½ cup of fresh raspberries.

6. Drizzle on the honey and garnish with the fresh mint. Serve surrounded by fresh fruits and/or other bite-size desserts.

Finishing

Italian Breadsticks	128	Beet Hummus	143
All the Pretty Carbs	131	Baked Brie	144
Red & Black Hummus	132	Dried Oranges	147
Tropical Guacamole	135	Spiced Pumpkin Seeds	148
Whipped Dip	136	Candied Pecans	151
G.O.A.T. Roasted Tomato Dip	139	Peanut Butter Frosting	152
Southern Pimento Cheese	140		

Touches

Italian Breadsticks

MAKES 18 BREADSTICKS

Breadsticks, often called grissini, are an Italian staple perfect for dipping into hummus, jam, soft cheese, herb butters—or simply devouring in all their naked glory. While you can buy Italian breadsticks at just about any grocery store, homemade grissini lend a special touch to your platters. Plus, rolling the dough is just like playing with play dough—get the kids involved or feel like a big kid yourself.

1¼ cups flour

2 teaspoons sugar

1½ teaspoons baking powder

½ teaspoon salt

¾ cup nondairy milk of your choice

2–3 tablespoons melted butter or olive oil

2–3 teaspoons sea salt

1. In a large bowl, combine the flour, sugar, baking powder, and salt. Add the milk and stir until a dough forms.

2. Knead the dough into a disk shape; wrap in plastic wrap. Place in the refrigerator for 30 minutes.

3. Preheat the oven to 450°F.

4. Remove the dough from the refrigerator. On a floured cutting board, roll out the dough into ¼-inch thickness.

5. Cut the dough into strips with a knife or pastry scraper. Roll between your hands to make a rope.

6. Place on a parchment-lined baking sheet. Brush with the melted butter or olive oil and bake for 10 to 15 minutes, or until golden brown.

7. Sprinkle with the sea salt before serving.

Style Points

Make a trendy twist. After you cut the grissini dough into strips, you can twist two strips together to make a bread braid. Add 2 to 3 minutes to the baking time for braids.

All the Pretty Carbs

SERVES 4–6 | USES 9" SQUARE TIN

Get rid of the cracker boxes and plastic sleeves! Elevate the experience with a tin or basket filled with pretty crackers and rustic bread to pair with your platters. Taro chips and rosemary croccantini crackers are must-haves in your ready-for-platters pantry.

22–24 multiseed crackers

14 taro chips

38–40 rosemary flatbread crackers (I recommend La Panzanella Rosemary Croccantini Crackers)

1 French baguette, warmed and sliced

Edible flowers and herbs, for garnish

1. Line a tin or basket with parchment paper.

2. Have fun filling with bread, crackers, and chips!

3. Tuck in edible flowers and herbs to garnish.

Red & Black Hummus

SERVES 4–6

Hummus is an absolutely quintessential Middle Eastern dip that is healthy, versatile, and delicious. Smoky and creamy, this roasted red pepper version will be a great addition to your grazes and spreads, and it's super easy to make with the help of a jar of roasted red peppers and a secret ingredient: black truffle salt.

1 (15-ounce) can chickpeas, rinsed and drained

¾ cup chopped roasted red peppers

¾ cup tahini paste

1 clove garlic

3 tablespoons lemon juice

2–3 tablespoons cold water

1 teaspoon black truffle salt

⅓ cup olive oil

Sea salt to taste

Basil leaf, for garnish

1. In a food processor, place the chickpeas, red peppers, tahini, garlic, lemon juice, cold water, and black truffle salt; blend.

2. While blending, drizzle in the olive oil and blend until smooth.

3. Spoon the hummus into a low-profile bowl, make a hummus swirl (see page 26 for directions), and top with the sea salt. Garnish with the basil leaf.

4. Serve with warm pita bread, cheese and crackers, or vegetables.

Tropical Guacamole

Creamy tropical guac is absolutely going to top your cravings list! Tropical avocados have a slightly sweeter flavor and lighter texture than other varieties. If you have never seen one IRL, you may be shocked by their size—tropical avocados are equivalent to four Hass avocados! Less prep for all that flavor.

1 tropical avocado (see tip below)

Juice of 1 or 2 limes

3 tablespoons chopped fresh cilantro

¼ sweet yellow onion, diced

Salt to taste

1. Cut the avocado in half and remove the pit. Scrape out the flesh into a medium bowl and mash with a fork.

2. Add the lime juice (reserving a squirt), cilantro, and onion and mash until smooth and creamy.

3. Top with a squirt of lime juice and a dash of salt to keep the top green.

4. Serve immediately or store in an airtight container in the refrigerator for up to 3 days. If storing, top with another squirt of lime juice.

Taste Tip

Make a simple swap. While it may be difficult to find tropical avocados in your area, you can get them via an online subscription box. I recommend Tropical Fruit Box for your avocado needs. Or feel free to swap out the tropical avocado with three or four fruits of a smaller, more common avocado variety.

Whipped Dip

SERVES 4–6

This light yet satisfying dip is perfect for brunch spreads
and as an anytime complement for fruits. Who can argue with four ingredients
and three steps to fab? If only everything in life were so easy!

4 ounces honey goat cheese, softened

1 (8-ounce) package cream cheese, softened

3 tablespoons raspberry fruit spread

3 tablespoons honey

1. In a bowl, whip together the goat cheese and cream cheese until smooth.

2. Fold in the raspberry fruit spread and honey.

3. Serve with fruit and your favorite breakfast carbs.

G.O.A.T. Roasted Tomato Dip

Here's a dip that deserves a standing invitation to all of your get-togethers. It's a party regular in our house—friends and family request its presence on the serving table and also the recipe to take along. Serve warm with lots of delicious crusty bread and crackers or veggies.

1 (8-ounce) package cream cheese, softened

4 ounces plain goat cheese, softened

¼ cup grated Parmesan cheese

2 tablespoons olive oil, divided

2 teaspoons sun-dried tomato pesto

2 teaspoons garlic powder

2 teaspoons onion powder

16–18 grape tomatoes, halved

½ clove garlic, thinly sliced

¼ cup shredded Parmesan cheese

Salt and freshly ground black pepper to taste

1. Preheat the oven to 400°F.

2. In a medium bowl, combine the cream cheese, goat cheese, and grated Parmesan cheese. Mix until well combined.

3. Add 1 tablespoon of the olive oil and the pesto, garlic powder, and onion powder to the cheese mixture; stir until creamy.

4. Smooth the dip into a baking dish and top with the tomatoes, garlic, remaining olive oil, shredded Parmesan cheese, and salt and pepper.

5. Bake for 15 to 20 minutes, or until the tomatoes are wilted and the top is lightly browned. Serve immediately.

Taste Tip

Spice it up. If you're like me and love a little heat, try adding a light dusting of cayenne and red pepper flakes with a dash of hot sauce for a spicy upgrade to your dip!

Southern Pimento Cheese

SERVES 4–6

This simple southern spread is a total treat at every gathering big or small. Don't tell anyone, but I love it baked too! The key to the perfect, authentic flavor is plenty of freshly shredded sharp cheddar and those classic jarred pimentos.

8 ounces cream cheese, softened

8 ounces shredded sharp cheddar

8 ounces shredded Mexican cheese

½ cup vegan mayo

3 or 4 pimentos, chopped

2 tablespoons white vinegar

¼ teaspoon cayenne pepper or red pepper flakes

Salt and freshly ground black pepper to taste

1. In a bowl, mix the cream cheese with the cheddar and Mexican cheeses until well combined.

2. Add the mayo, pimentos, vinegar, cayenne pepper, and salt and pepper.

3. Serve with crackers, bread, or raw vegetables.

Beet Hummus

Vibrant beet hummus will get your guests oohing and aahing with excitement and curiosity. But it's more than the color that stands out. The orange-infused olive oil and za'atar seasoning take the flavor to a whole new level. While it may seem fancy, the hummus is crazy easy to make, with 99.9 percent of the work done by your food processor.

1 (15-ounce) can chickpeas, rinsed and drained

1 (8.8-ounce) package cooked beets (I recommend Love Beets)

¾ cup tahini paste

1 clove garlic

3 tablespoons lemon juice

2–3 tablespoons cold water or 1 or 2 ice cubes

3 teaspoons sea salt, divided

2–3 tablespoons orange-infused olive oil, divided

1–2 tablespoons honey, for garnish

1 tablespoon za'atar seasoning, for garnish

3 tablespoons diced candied orange peel

1–2 tablespoons honeycomb, for garnish

1–2 tablespoons microgreens, for garnish

1 or 2 purple radishes, sliced, for garnish and dipping

1. In a food processor, place the chickpeas, beets, tahini, garlic, lemon juice, cold water, and 2 teaspoons of the sea salt; blend.

2. While blending, drizzle in 2 tablespoons of the olive oil and blend until smooth.

3. Spoon the hummus into a low-profile bowl and top with the remaining olive oil. Garnish with the honey, za'atar seasoning, remaining sea salt, candied orange peel, honeycomb, and microgreens.

4. Serve with purple radishes, pita bread topped with more za'atar seasoning, and additional raw vegetables.

Baked Brie

Introducing baked Brie, the ultimate comfort food to add to your grazing spreads. Brie is super versatile and can be eaten with a wide variety of pairings. Top with a simple combo of fruit spread, nuts, and honey, and you really can't go wrong. Try scoring the top rind of the Brie wheel instead of cutting it off—it's completely edible and adds a nice texture and flavor to the dish.

1 (8-ounce) Brie wheel

3–4 tablespoons apricot fruit spread

1 Bosc pear, sliced

2 ounces ghost pepper (or your favorite hot) honey, divided (I recommend Naturacentric)

¼ cup chopped pistachios, divided

1. Preheat the oven to 400°F.

2. Score the top of the Brie with a paring knife. Place in the skillet.

3. Top with the apricot spread, pear slices, 1 ounce of the honey, and 2 tablespoons of the pistachios.

4. Bake for 15 to 20 minutes, or until melty.

5. Top with the remaining honey and pistachios. Serve immediately with crackers or bread.

Dried Oranges

MAKES 40 SLICES

Vibrant colors, interesting shapes, and cool textures are what make platters total eye candy for your guests. Garnish with natural ingredients as often as you can, like with these pretty dried oranges. Simply slice and bake on low to create gorgeous toppers for cheeses and dips and fantastic fillers for gaps and corners on your boards. I adore blood oranges, but you can dry any kind you like.

4 blood oranges, thinly sliced

2 tablespoons sugar (optional)

1. Preheat the oven to 200°F. Spray a baking sheet with cooking spray.

2. Slice the oranges and arrange on the baking sheet. Sprinkle lightly with the sugar, if using.

3. Bake for 2 to 2½ hours, turning occasionally and checking frequently in the last hour. Store in an airtight container for up to a week.

Spiced Pumpkin Seeds

MAKES 2 CUPS

It doesn't take mastering four-course meals to feel like a Michelin-star chef! Try simply making your own toasted nuts or seeds to add to your boards and platters. A basic pantry item can become something spectacular with a little time in the skillet and the right seasonings.

1 tablespoon olive oil

2 cups pumpkin seeds

2–3 teaspoons toast sugar (see tip below)

1. Heat the oil in a medium skillet over medium heat.

2. Add the pumpkin seeds to the skillet.

3. Toast for about 5 minutes, stirring frequently to keep from burning.

4. Remove from the heat and place in a bowl. Sprinkle with the toast sugar.

Taste Tip

Discover toast sugar. I recommend Portland Salt Co for this yummy blend of vanilla sugar, cinnamon, sea salt, molasses, and nutmeg. A dash makes a delicious difference on so many foods! You'll find yourself reaching for it all the time.

Candied Pecans

MAKES 4 CUPS

Candied pecans are the perfect addition to your platters and boards! They roast up quickly in the oven with just a few ingredients you likely have on hand. You can look for vegan butter and use 2 tablespoons of aquafaba (liquid drained from chickpeas) in place of the egg white to make these strictly plant-based.

½ stick unsalted butter, cut into slices

1 egg white

4 cups pecans

¾ cup sugar

1 tablespoon cinnamon

Pinch of salt

Sea salt to taste

1. Preheat the oven to 325°F.

2. Place the butter on a baking sheet and warm in the oven until melted, about 5 to 10 minutes.

3. In a large bowl or bowl of a stand mixer, whip the egg white until frothy.

4. Toss the pecans with the egg white until evenly coated.

5. In a separate bowl, combine the sugar, cinnamon, and salt. Add the sugar mixture to the nuts.

6. Transfer the nuts to the baking sheet with the melted butter. Gently fold together the butter and nuts.

7. Roast for up to 45 minutes, flipping the pecans at least once during baking.

8. Remove from the oven and sprinkle with sea salt. Allow to cool before serving. Or store in an airtight container at room temperature for up to 1 week, refrigerated up to 3 weeks, or frozen for up to 2 months.

Peanut Butter Frosting

MAKES 2 CUPS

This frosting is the icing on the cake . . . or brownie or cookie or crispy rice treat! It's also a delicious offering to serve with fruit, graham crackers, and pretzels. Trust me, when you make it, it won't go to waste.

1 cup unsalted butter, softened

1 cup creamy peanut butter

½ cup powdered sugar

1 teaspoon vanilla extract

1. In a medium mixing bowl or work bowl of a stand mixer, whip together the butter and peanut butter.

2. Add the powdered sugar a little at a time and whip until combined, then mix in the vanilla.

3. Enjoy immediately or store in a sealed container in the fridge for up to a week. Before using, let the frosting come to room temperature to soften up for spreading.

Index

A

acorn squash bowl, 116, 117
  how to make, 117
All the Pretty Carbs, 131
almonds
  dill pickle, 30, 57
  Marcona, 42, 43, 96, 97, 113,
    121, 122
  pumpkin creme, 116, 117
  rosemary, 34
  smoked, 37
  truffle Marcona, 26
Always Hummus, 34
anytime grazing platters and
  boards
  Always Hummus, 34
  Big Softy, 30
  Caprese Dream, 42–43
  Cookie Cutie, 61
  Crabby but Cute, 54
  Crudités Canvas, 38
  Date Night In, 49
  DIY Crostini, 53
  Everyday Royalty, 26
  Gouda for You, 37
  Manchego River, 41
  New Classic Cheese Balls,
    58
  Papayeah Platter, 46
  Pretty in Parmesan, 33
  Sunday Best, 50
  Sweet Hot Honey, 45

Swirl Girl, 29
Takeout Snack Baskets, 57
Appetizer Pizza, 82
appetizer serving sizes, 15
apple balls, dried, 61
apples, 109
  Fuji, 68, 106, 107
  Gala, 121
  Granny Smith, 30, 106, 107,
    110, 111
  red, 102
  rose, 67, 85
applewood smoked sea salt,
  71, 72
apricot fruit spread, 106, 107,
  144
apricots, dried, 26, 29, 37, 41,
  45, 50, 61, 68, 93, 106, 107,
  110, 111, 113, 116, 117
arugula, 68, 75, 109
asparagus, 38, 78, 79, 82, 114
avocados, 41, 64, 68, 71, 72,
  82, 94, 96, 97
  ripeness test for, 20
  tropical, 135

B

baguettes, 78, 79, 110, 111, 131.
  See also crostini
Baked Brie, 144
balsamic glaze, 53, 75
balsamic vinaigrette, 67, 72

basil, 82
  for garnish, 29, 30, 33, 38,
    41, 42, 46, 57, 67, 75, 106,
    107, 109, 113, 114, 132
bee pollen, 46, 106, 107
beet hummus, 29
  recipe, 143
beet tortillas, 98
Berries, Balsamic & Butter, 72
Best Baked Feta, 89
Big Softy, 30
black bean burger patties, 93
blackberries, 26, 29, 30, 41,
  45, 49, 53, 67, 102, 109
  Berries, Balsamic & Butter,
    72
blackberry jelly, 45
blackberry mulled merlot jam,
  113
black truffle salt, 132
blueberries, 29, 41, 54, 68,
  93, 102
  Berries, Balsamic & Butter,
    72
blue cheese
  about, 16
  cave-aged, 26, 30, 116, 117
  creamy soft-ripened, 78, 79
  plain, 49
  vegan, 110, 111
blue cheese spread, 53
bolillo rolls, 94
Boursin cheese, 75

bowls, 11, 12, 19
bread. *See also* baguettes
  olive, 110, 111
bread slices, 96, 97
breadsticks. *See* Italian
  breadsticks
Brie
  Baked Brie, 144
  Brie Mine, 85
  double crème, 116, 117
  triple crème, 110, 111
Bring It to the Table, 113
broccoli, 78, 79
broccolini, 106, 107
brownies, 118
  PB & Brownie Party, 122
buttered toast crackers, 116,
  117
butter lettuce, 68, 72, 98
butternut squash gnocchi, 71

C

Candied Pecans, 151
candy canes, 105, 118
Caprese Dream, 42–43
carrot fronds, for garnish, 118
carrots, 106, 107
  baby, 29, 38
  rainbow, 93, 114
cashew cheese
  French-style, 38
  vegan, 86
  vegan chive, 30
cashews, 105, 110, 111
  coconut, 29, 30, 54
  honey-roasted, 49
  sesame-honey, 49
  Thai curry, 34
cauliflower, 42, 43, 75, 82,
  86, 90, 114
  Crispy Cauliflower Wraps,
  98
cayenne pepper, 98, 140
celery, 75
Chao cheese, vegan, 98, 105

Charcuterie Cones, 105
cheddar
  aged white, 57, 110, 111
  balsamic and cipollini aged,
  50
  medium, 30
  mild, 57
  pink, 113
  sharp, 96, 97, 140
  sharp white, 53
  smoked, 26, 110, 111
  vegan white, 41
  Vino Rosso aged white, 116,
  117
  white, 58, 96, 97, 109
  wine-soaked, 42, 43, 78, 79
cheese. *See also specific*
  cheeses
  Baked Brie, 144
  Best Baked Feta, 89
  Cheese Battle, 86
  G.O.A.T. Roasted Tomato
  Dip, 139
  Gouda for You, 37
  Grown-Up Grilled Cheese,
  96–97
  Manchego River, 41
  New Classic Cheese Balls,
  58
  placement of, 16
  Pretty in Parmesan, 33
  Southern Pimento Cheese,
  140
  Sweet, Spicy & Cheesy, 90
  types of, 15, 16
Cheese Battle, 86
cheese curds, garlic, 50
cheese knives, 12
cheese roses, how to make,
  109
cheese stars, how to make,
  67
cherries
  dried, 33
  red, 26, 102

Chex Mix Muddy Buddies,
  102
"chicken" patties, 94
chickpea masala dip, 42, 43
chickpeas, 71, 86, 90, 132, 143
chickpea salad, 75
chili lime seasoning, for garnish, 34
chipotle almond dip or
  spread, 34, 78, 79, 98
chive cashew cheese, 30
chocolate bar, 118
chocolate peppermint sandwich cookies, 118
cilantro, 68, 72, 86, 89, 98,
  135
  for garnish, 71, 80, 81, 93
cinnamon sugar, 122
clementines, 30, 116, 117
coconut cashews, 29, 30, 54
coconut strips, dried, 29, 54
collard greens, 90
Cookie Cutie, 61
cookies
  chocolate peppermint
  sandwich, 118
  maple sandwich, 61
  pumpkin spice sandwich,
  116, 117
  sugar, 118
  vanilla wafer, 105
corn cobs, baby, 114
cornichons, 41, 50, 53, 94,
  96, 97, 116, 117
Couscous, A Pop of, 71
Crabby but Cute, 54
crackers
  buttered toast, 116, 117
  flatbread, 57, 89
  fruit and nut, 86, 116, 117, 121
  multiseed, 131
  pita, 30
  pumpkin seed, 45
  rosemary, 37, 58, 109
  rosemary flatbread, 29, 85,
  131

savory rice, 106, 107
sesame, 50, 54
sprouted wheat, 29, 54, 109
three-seed beet, 110, 111
water, 41, 49, 113
cranberries, dried, 26, 49, 50, 109, 113
   Stars & Cranberries, 67
cream cheese, 136, 139, 140
   vegan, 58
Crispy Cauliflower Wraps, 98
crostini, 30, 37, 53, 85, 89
   buttered, 42, 43
   customizing, 43
   DIY Crostini, 53
   herbed, 42, 43
   homemade, 33, 34
crudités
   Crowd-Pleasing Crudités, 114
   Crudités Canvas, 38
cucumbers, 37, 116, 117
   English, 26, 38, 42, 43, 57, 72, 96, 97, 106, 107, 110, 111, 114
   Persian, 38, 109

D
Date Night In, 49
decorative trays and baskets, 12
desserts. See sweets and celebrations
Dijon vinaigrette, 64
dill, for garnish, 38, 71
dinner serving sizes, 15
dips and spreads
   chipotle almond, 34, 78, 79, 98
   G.O.A.T. Roasted Tomato Dip, 139
   Southern Pimento Cheese, 140
   tofu, 78, 79, 110, 111
   types of, 15

Whipped Dip, 136
dishes
   choosing, 11, 12
   placement of, 19
DIY Crostini, 53
dragon fruit, 46
dried fruits
   apple balls, 61
   apricots, 26, 29, 37, 41, 45, 50, 61, 68, 93, 106, 107, 110, 111, 113, 116, 117
   cherries, 33
   coconut strips, 29, 54
   cranberries, 26, 49, 50, 67, 109, 113
   figs, 26, 34, 41, 72, 116, 117
   mangoes, 29, 33, 45, 49, 110, 111
   oranges, 29, 54, 109, 121, 147
   placement of, 23
   tangerines, 49, 61, 113, 122

E
Eat Beautifully method, 16, 19–20, 23
Eat the Rainbow, 106–7
edamame, 38, 42, 43, 114
edible flowers, for garnish, 23, 29, 33, 41, 45, 49, 50, 61, 105, 109, 110, 111, 113, 116, 117, 118, 121, 122, 131
endive, 29, 38, 114
Everyday Royalty, 26
everything-but-the-bagel seasoning, 38, 86, 94

F
Fajita Flavor, 80–81
fajita seasoning, homemade, 80, 81
feta cheese, 90
   Best Baked Feta, 89
   crumbles, 64, 78, 79, 96, 97

sun-dried tomato, 80, 81
feta dressing, 57, 93
figs, dried, 26, 34, 41, 72, 116, 117
flatbread crackers, 57, 89
flowers. See edible flowers, for garnish
food labels, 12
fresh cheeses, 16
Friends & Family Circle, 110–11
fruit and nut crackers, 86, 116, 117, 121
fruits. See also dried fruits; specific fruits
   choosing, 19–20
   fancy cutting of, 21
   seasonal, 20
   suggested, 15

G
garlic, 64, 89, 132, 139, 143
garlic and herb cheese, 54, 82
garlic cheese curds, 50
garlic powder, 98, 139
garnishes. See also edible flowers, for garnish; specific herbs
   placement of, 23
Gifts of Grazing, 121
gluten-free flour, 98
gnocchi, butternut squash, 71
goat cheese
   blueberry-vanilla, 68, 106, 107, 110, 111
   chocolate chip, 30
   cranberry, 30, 67, 110, 111
   cranberry-cinnamon, 45, 72
   herbed, 116, 117
   honey, 136
   plain, 50, 86, 90, 106, 107, 110, 111, 116, 117, 139
   G.O.A.T. Roasted Tomato Dip, 139
gooseberries, 46

Gorgonzola, 49, 58, 106, 107
Gouda, 37, 50, 94
grapes
  green, 41, 96, 97, 106, 107
  purple, 116, 117
  red, 67, 72, 102, 110, 111, 116,
    117
Grazing Cane, 109
grazing table, 11
green beans, 96, 97, 114
Grown-Up Grilled Cheese,
  96–97
guacamole, 80, 81
  Tropical Guacamole, 135
guavas, 46
  cutting, 21
gumdrops, 118
gummies
  lips, 118
  peach ring, 113, 116, 117
  vegan bears, 105

H
habanero pepper jelly, 90
Happily Avo After, 68
hard cheeses, 16
Havarti, 49, 121
  dill, 75, 102, 121
  vegan, 34
herbs, for garnish, 23. *See
  also specific herbs*
honey, 58, 136
  clover, 33
  cranberry, 26, 67, 110, 111
  for garnish, 143
  ghost pepper, 68, 106, 107,
    144
  habanero, 45
  Meyer lemon, 30
  Mission fig, 33, 41, 49
  rosemary-infused, 64, 125
  sage and walnut, 113
  Valencia orange, 46, 106,
    107

vanilla-cinnamon, 37, 72,
  116, 117
honeycomb, for garnish, 143
honey mustard, 94, 98
honey-mustard dressing, 68
Hot Cocoa Bomb Board, 118
hot pepper jelly, 26
hot platters
  Appetizer Pizza, 82
  Best Baked Feta, 89
  Brie Mine, 85
  Cheese Battle, 86
  Crispy Cauliflower Wraps,
    98
  Fajita Flavor, 80–81
  Grown-Up Grilled Cheese,
    96–97
  Pita Party, 93
  Roasted Veggie Mezze,
    78–79
  Super Sandwiches, 94
  Sweet, Spicy & Cheesy, 90
hot sauce, 93
hummus
  Always Hummus, 34
  beet, 29
    recipe, 143
  garlic, 78, 79
  plain, 26, 34, 42, 43, 78, 79,
    110, 111
  Red & Black Hummus, 132
  red pepper, 37, 116, 117
  spicy, 98
  spicy yellow lentil, 50
  swirling, 26

I
ingredients
  order of placement, 16,
    19–20, 23
  planning, 15
Israeli couscous, 71
Italian breadsticks, 26, 33,
  42, 43, 53, 86
  recipe, 128

J
Jack cheese, 109
  pepper, 109
jalapeños, 80, 81

K
kitchen tools, 12, 19
kiwis, 116, 117
  cutting, 21
knives, cheese, 12
kumquats, 46

L
lavender, for garnish, 105
limes, 46, 68, 80, 81, 106,
  107, 135

M
Manchego, 34, 53, 93, 102,
  121
  Manchego River, 41
mangoes
  dried, 29, 33, 45, 49, 110, 111
  fresh, 46, 106, 107
  scoring, 21
mango rose, 29, 45, 49
maple sandwich cookies, 61
marble platters, 12
Marcona almonds, 42, 43,
  96, 97, 113, 121, 122
marinara, 96, 97
marionberries, 45, 72
marionberry-habanero jelly,
  110, 111, 116, 117
marshmallows, 118
mascarpone cheese, 125
"meal" boards, 16
meats, order of placement
  for, 16
Medjool date bars, 29
Medjool dates, 30, 33, 49,
  68, 106, 107, 121, 122
Mexican cheese, 80, 81, 140

microgreens, 53, 58, 93
  for garnish, 38, 46, 96, 97,
    110, 111, 114, 143
mint, for garnish, 30, 64, 93,
  125
mozzarella, vegan, 42, 43
multiseed crackers, 131
mushrooms, 86, 93, 114
mustard
  Dijon, 64
  honey, 94, 98
  whole-grain yellow, 42, 43

N

napkins, 12
natural stone platters, 12
New Classic Cheese Balls, 58
nuts. *See also specific nuts*
  mixed, 30, 113
  placement of, 23

O

olive bread, 110, 111
olive oil, 34, 64, 67, 68, 72,
  75, 80, 81, 82, 86, 89, 90,
  132, 139, 148
  orange-infused, 143
olives
  black, 53, 82
  blue cheese-stuffed, 116, 117
  Castelvetrano, 26, 75
  garlic-stuffed, 30, 93, 96,
    97
  green, 42, 43, 78, 79, 86
  marinated, 34, 53
  pimento-stuffed, 105
onion powder, 98, 139
onions, 78, 79, 80, 81, 82, 135
onion topping, caramelized,
  53
orange peel, candied, 143
oranges, 37, 49, 94, 113
  blood, 46, 106, 107
  Cara Cara, 53, 106, 107

dried, 29, 54, 109, 121
  recipe, 147
navel, 45, 68, 85, 122
oregano, for garnish, 110, 111,
  121

P

pantry items
  placement of, 23
  types of, 15
panzanella salad, 53
papayas, mini, 46, 106, 107
Papayeah Platter, 46
paprika, smoked, 58
parchment paper, 12
Parmesan cheese, 64, 82,
  139
  Pretty in Parmesan, 33
Parmesan crisps, 26, 113
Parmesan toasts, 50
parsley, for garnish, 114
Patriotic Platter, 102
PB & Brownie Party, 122
peach ring gummies, 113, 116,
  117
peanut butter
  PB & Brownie Party, 122
  Peanut Butter Frosting, 152
peanut butter cups, 121
pears, 49, 144
peas, 71, 93
pecans, 58, 64, 71
  candied, 33, 67
    recipe, 151
  sweet and spicy, 33, 37, 41,
    85
peperoncini, 78, 79, 93, 96,
  97
pepper Jack cheese, 109
peppermint candies, 118
peppermint lollipops, 105
peppermint toffee candies, 118
peppers
  bell, 64, 75, 78, 79, 80, 81,
    106, 107

jalapeño, 80, 81
  mini sweet, 29, 38, 41, 50,
    90, 93, 96, 97, 106, 107,
    114, 116, 117
  stuffed, 57
  roasted red, 132
pesto, 42, 43
  sun-dried tomato, 139
pickles, 37, 78, 79, 110, 111
pie crust, 125
Pimento Cheese, Southern,
  140
pineapple ripeness test, 20
pistachio nut clusters, 34
pistachios, 30, 34, 37, 41, 50,
  64, 78, 79, 85, 94, 110, 111,
  144
pita crackers, 30
Pita Party, 93
Pizza, Appetizer, 82
plant-based cheeses, 16
plant-based ingredients,
  benefits of, 11
plant-forward eating, 9
platters and boards
  accessories for, 12
  choosing, 11–12
  Eat Beautifully method and,
    16, 19–20, 23
  ingredients for, 15
  shapes of, 12
  themes for, 11
  versatility of, 11
pomegranate, 116, 117
Pop of Couscous, A, 71
potato chips, jalapeño, 80, 81
potatoes, Yukon gold, 80, 81
Pretty in Parmesan, 33
Pretty Little Layers, 64
pretzels
  pretzel sticks, 34
  yogurt-covered, 102, 116,
    117, 118
provolone, 102
provolone roses, 80, 81, 109
puff pastry, 82

pumpkin pie spice, 58
pumpkin seed crackers, 45
Pumpkin Seeds, Spiced, 148
pumpkin spice sandwich
    cookies, 116, 117

R

radicchio, 38, 114
radicchio bowl, how to make,
    38
radishes, 29, 38, 42, 43, 50,
    57, 75, 86, 90, 93, 96, 97,
    114, 143
ramekins, 11, 12, 19
ranch dressing, 41, 42, 43,
    57, 96, 97, 114
raspberries, 49, 102, 110, 111,
    125
raspberry fruit spread, 136
raspberry-marionberry fruit
    spread, 30, 85, 122
Raspberry (S)tart, 125
Ready-for-Broadcast Board,
    116–17
Red & Black Hummus, 132
refried black beans, 80, 81
relish platter, for grilled
    cheese sandwiches, 96–97
Roasted Veggie Mezze,
    78–79
romaine lettuce, 42, 43, 94
Romano cheese, 96, 97, 113
rosemary, 121
    for garnish, 29, 41, 45, 50,
        53, 122
rosemary crackers, 37, 58,
    109
rosemary flatbread crackers,
    29, 85, 131

S

sage, for garnish, 33, 34, 38,
    45, 49, 50, 110, 111, 116, 117,
    121

sage Derby, 113
salad, panzanella, 53
salad spreads
    Berries, Balsamic & Butter,
        72
    Happily Avo After, 68
    A Pop of Couscous, 71
    Pretty Little Layers, 64
    Sheet Pan Sensation, 75
    Stars & Cranberries, 67
salami, 110, 111
salsa, chipotle, 80, 81
sandwiches
    Crispy Cauliflower Wraps,
        98
    grilled cheese sandwiches,
        96, 97
    Super Sandwiches, 94
savory rice crackers, 106, 107
scallions, 38, 71, 82, 89, 114
    for garnish, 78, 79
scrapbook paper cone, how
    to make, 105
sea salt, 122, 132, 143
seasonal ingredients, 15
semihard cheeses, 16
semisoft cheeses, 16
serving size guide, 15
serving tools, 12
sesame crackers, 50, 54
shallots, 72, 75, 89, 90
shapes, platter, 12
Sheet Pan Sensation, 75
small plates, 12
smoked paprika, 58
snap peas, 38
soft-ripened cheeses, 16
sour cream, 80, 81
Southern Pimento Cheese,
    140
Spiced Pumpkin Seeds, 148
spinach, 71, 80, 81
spreads. See dips and
    spreads
spring salad mix, 38, 42, 43,
    64, 67, 93, 114

sprouted wheat crackers, 29,
    54, 109
Stars & Cranberries, 67
steak salt, 93
strawberries, 46, 116, 117, 121,
    122
strawberry-habanero jelly,
    125
strawberry heart, how to
    make, 122
stroopwafels, 61
sugar cookies, 118
Sunday Best, 50
Super Sandwiches, 94
Sweet, Spicy & Cheesy, 90
Sweet Hot Honey, 45
sweets and celebrations
    Bring It to the Table, 113
    Charcuterie Cones, 105
    Crowd-Pleasing Crudités,
        114
    Eat the Rainbow, 106–7
    Friends & Family Circle,
        110–11
    Gifts of Grazing, 121
    Grazing Cane, 109
    Hot Cocoa Bomb Board, 118
    Patriotic Platter, 102
    PB & Brownie Party, 122
    Raspberry (S)tart, 125
    Ready-for-Broadcast Board,
        116–17
Swirl Girl, 29

T

taco shells, 80, 81
tahini paste, 132, 143
Takeout Snack Baskets, 57
tangelos, 110, 111
tangerines, 30, 110, 111
    dried, 49, 61, 113, 122
taralli, fennel, 57
taro chips, 131
tart
    Raspberry (S)tart, 125

three-seed beet crackers, 110, 111
thyme, for garnish, 33, 34, 85
toast sugar, 148
tofu-based dip, 110, 111
tofu spread, 78, 79
tomatoes
  cherry, 113, 116, 117
  grape, 42, 43, 53, 64, 75, 78, 79, 80, 81, 82, 89, 96, 97, 98, 102, 109, 110, 111, 114, 121, 139
  green marinated, 53
  Roma, 42, 43, 80, 81
  on the vine, 89, 94
tongs, 12
tortillas, beet, 98
trail mix, 110, 111, 113
Tropical Guacamole, 135
truffle oil, 58
truffles, dark chocolate, 118
truffle salt, 75, 132
turkey, 105
tzatziki, 110, 111
  vegan, 42, 43, 114

U

unconventional boards, 12
unconventional charcuterie, 121

V

vanilla wafer cookies, 105
vegan cheeses
  blue, 110, 111
  cashew cheese, 86
  Chao, 98, 105
  Charcuterie Cones, 105
  chive cashew, 30
  cream cheese, 58
  French-style cashew, 38
  garlic and herb spread, 54
  Havarti, 34
  mozzarella, 42, 43

  Parmesan, 64
  types of, 16
  white cheddar, 41
vegan mayo, 94, 140
vegan tzatziki, 42, 43, 114
vegetables. *See also* crudités; *specific vegetables*
  choosing, 19–20
  Roasted Veggie Mezze, 78–79
  roasting, 79, 80, 81
  seasonal, 20
  suggested, 15
  veggie sticks, 94
vinaigrettes
  balsamic, 67, 72
  Dijon, 64

W

walnuts, 49, 68, 85, 113, 122
washed-rind cheeses, 16
water crackers, 41, 49, 113
watermelon, 102
Whipped Dip, 136
wood boards, 11–12

Y

yogurt, 46
yogurt-covered pretzels, 102, 116, 117, 118

Z

za'atar, 30, 78, 79, 143
zucchini, 78, 79, 80, 81, 106, 107